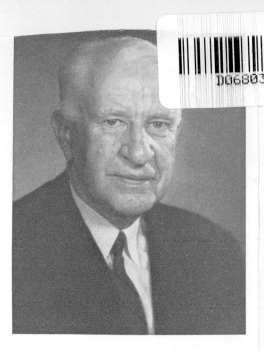

JOHN E. MITCHELL, JR., is president
of a Dallas, Texas, machinery manufacturing company which bears his name
and which has attained international
recognition for its outstanding in-plant
religious program. Chairman of the
Dallas Theological Seminary Board of
Trustees, a director of the Dallas Bible
Institute and a national director in the
Young Life Campaign, he is a former
president of the Dallas Citizens Council,
vice president of both the Dallas Cham-
ber of Commerce and the Greater Dallas
Planning Council, board member of
Southern Methodist University's Graduate Research Center, and director of
both Austin and Wheaton Colleges.
Mr. Mitchell has long been active in the
First Presbyterian Church of Dallas,
serving this congregation as an elder and
as Sunday school teacher. *The Christian
in Business* is his first book.

The
Christian
in
Business

John E. Mitchell, Jr.

The

Christian

in

Business

FLEMING H. REVELL COMPANY

Two of my closest business associates and most intimate friends are stalwart Christians. As such, they have greatly influenced my own life. It is to them, my brothers Orville and Donald, that this book is gratefully and affectionately dedicated.

PREFACE

The reader of this book will notice that practically all of the illustrations used come from experiences in my own company. I shall not apologize for this, because it is just about all I know.

Except for three months spent as a cost "expert" in a shoe-heel factory at age nineteen, I have worked only for one firm all my life. This firm was founded by my father about 1900 under the name of the Mitchell-Parks Manufacturing Company. In 1905 its name was changed to the Alsop Process Company and finally, in 1922, it took its present name, the John E. Mitchell Company.

I have put in about 105,000 working hours with the company: first as an apprentice in the machine shop, then successively as an office worker, Vice President (1920 to 1938), President (1938 to 1962) and now Chairman of the Board (1962-   ).

It has been an exhilarating, exciting experience and I am grateful for every minute of it. I am grateful for the good and the bad—for the frequent disappointments and setbacks as well as the occasional accomplishments and successes. I am particularly thankful to the Lord for all the fine people He has permitted me to know and to associate with, in the office, in the factory, in the field, among customers, suppliers, competitors, government people, neighbors —some of them still here, others gone.

If this book will encourage a few men and women to put more into their work and therefore to get more

7

out of it; if it will cause the Christians who read it to remember that God has called them to their jobs and expects them to perform their work "heartily, as to the Lord"; if it will impress upon Christian managers that they are stewards of God and servants of stockholders, customers, employees, suppliers and neighbors; and if—above all else—it may create in someone the desire to come into intimate fellowship with our wonderful Lord Himself, then this book will have served its purpose and we shall consider that our work upon it has not been in vain.

John E. Mitchell, Jr.

Dallas, Texas

CONTENTS

CONTENTS

9

The
    Christian
in
    Business

PERSON-to-PERSON

WILL RELIGION AND BUSINESS MIX? Is God interested in the way we do our work?

Is He interested in a lathe operator and in the quantity and quality of his output? Is He interested in a watchman as he makes his rounds through the warehouse in the darkness and silence of the night? Is He interested in a stenographer and the way she types her letters? Is He interested in a salesman and what he says to a prospect?

Is God concerned about a businessman's business? Is God there when he makes out his expense account or his income tax return? Does He take an interest in the company's advertising campaign and the claims made for the company's products? Is He present at personal interviews, and at our conferences, directors meetings, labor union negotiations, trade conventions, business lunches and black-tie banquets?

When a businessman succeeds or fails, is God interested? Does He care how a man takes his disappointments and his failures? How success is achieved? How a man weathers prosperity?

In short, does God belong in business? Should he be the businessman's Advisor? his Consultant? his Confidant? his silent Partner?

To say "No" to these questions is to relegate God to a place of no importance in that very area of a man's life where he spends most of his waking hours

—at the store, the factory, the office, wherever he earns his living. To say "No" is to deny the Lord the preëminent place in our lives that He demands and, instead, to put Him on the shelf as the heathen does with his gods of wood and stone, to be taken down only in an emergency. A Sunday God is no God at all.

On the other hand, he who answers "Yes" to these questions and who bases the pursuit of his career upon that answer, whether he be a Supreme Court Justice or a garbage collector, transforms that career into a thing of dignity, high purpose, satisfaction and excitement. A Christian's work should be far more than a mere livelihood; it is an opportunity to honor God by its performance. By his attitude toward his work, by the spirit in which he performs it, a Christian—whether he be employer or employee—should be a good advertisement, not so much for himself as for the Master.

Jesus said: "Let your light so shine before men that they may see your good works, and glorify your Father which is in heaven" (Matthew 5:16). How can we glorify the Father? By the fervent singing of hymns on Sunday? By teaching a Sunday school class? By making our contributions when the collection plate is passed? Yes, of course; but also, and especially, as Christians by dedicating our jobs to Christ, and by performing our work—every detail of it—honestly, faithfully, unselfishly, enthusiastically, in a manner that will please Him. It should be possible to identify a Christian merely by watching him at his daily task.

Many years ago, in a little manufacturing company now much larger and fairly successful, there were two

employees—one, a shipping clerk named Matlock
and the other a night janitor named Washam. One
of Washam's duties was to clean out the big brass
cuspidors in the various offices. This was an onerous
job, because in those days there was much tobacco
chewing; and due to carelessness, poor marksmanship, and the nature of the commodity, the spittoons
were usually filthy. One of the spittoons belonged to
Matlock, a crotchety chap who took pride in his own
work and was ready and quick to criticize what he
regarded as poor work by another. Matlock became
dissatisfied with the job Washam was doing on his
cuspidor and told him so in a note which he attached one evening to the offending object. This note
led to various exchanges, and a bitter feeling between
the two men soon developed. The disagreement finally reached the point where neither would speak
to the other when they chanced to meet in the evening.

The president of the company heard about the
matter and decided to deal first with Washam. Accordingly, he remained at the plant one night to talk
to the janitor on the job.

"Brother Washam," said the president, "I am
greatly disappointed in you. You and I belong to the
same church. We both profess to be Christians.
Surely Christ would not be pleased with this silly
quarrel over a cuspidor. Now, here is what I want
you to do," he went on; "I want you to make Matlock's cuspidor the Number One item on your program every night. I want you to clean it and polish
it as no cuspidor has ever been cleaned and polished
before. I am going to stay here tonight long enough
to help you with it myself. Let's remember that we

are doing this job not for Matlock, but for the Lord.
I believe the Lord has a special interest in this particular cuspidor. Let's do a really good job for Him."

Thus encouraged, the janitor went to work immediately on Matlock's brass cuspidor, and in half
an hour it was a shining thing of beauty. In fact,
Matlock could see the reflection of his face in its sur-
face when he looked at it early the next morning.
Matlock was greatly surprised. But especially was he
surprised when he learned what had happened the
night before; also he was embarrassed and ashamed.
When the president brought the two men together
in his office, they confessed that they had been acting
like spoiled children. They shook hands then and
there and began a friendship that endured for the
rest of their lives.

Washam, Matlock and the president of the company have gone from the scene now these many
years, but the symbol of the shining brass cuspidor
lives on in the company they worked for. If you
should visit the company today, you would notice on
the walls of the different departments in all the factory buildings, and on all the desks in all the company's offices, a framed motto with these words
printed in gold letters:

> "And whatsoever ye do, do it heartily, as to the Lord,
> and not unto men" (Colossians 3:23).

I recommend that motto as a basis for every Christian's business life, and for every company that pro-
fesses to be Christian in its policies and activities.

The Christian religion, to have any merit or any
life, must be a Person-to-person relationship. Indeed,
a Christian is merely one who has accepted Christ

as his personal Saviour, as the Lord of his life, and as his closest Friend with whom he can share his problems, adversities, failures, successes and prosperity. One of the most thrilling discoveries that a man can make is to learn, first from a reading of the Scriptures and then from actual practical experience in his own life, that Christ loves *him* and is interested in *him,* personally.

The Scriptures abound in assurances of this personal relationship. Consider, for example, just three of them:

"Behold, I stand at the door, and knock: if any man hear my voice, and open the door, I will come in to him, and will sup with him, and he with me" (Revelation 3:20).

"Peace I leave with you, my peace I give unto you: not as the world giveth, give I unto you. Let not your heart be troubled, neither let it be afraid" (John 14: 27).

"In my Father's house are many mansions: if it were not so, I would have told you. I go to prepare a place for you. And if I go and prepare a place for you, I will come again, and receive you unto myself; that where I am, there ye may be also" (John 14:2, 3).

I see no great problem in the fact that I am only one of more than two billion people living on this earth at the present time; that the earth is just one planet revolving around the sun, ninety-three million miles away; that the sun is only one of several million suns, or stars, in our galaxy; that our galaxy is only one of several million such galaxies. Neither am I unduly concerned when they tell me that there are 3,000,000,000,000,000,000,000 atoms in a gram of gold, and that each of these atoms is a cosmos in itself, a system characterized by inconceivably vast "interplanetary" spaces. God is not only God of the galaxy, and God of the atom; He is also my God and according to His Word, loves me personally, and is interested in everything I do and say and think.

To quote a very simple but beautiful song that our children sing in Sunday school: "Jesus loves me; this I know, for the Bible tells me so."

Not only does the Bible tell us so, but we find it out from personal experience as we put God's words to the test in our lives on a person-to-Person basis. Any Christian who has had this kind of intimate experience with Him can testify that the Lord *is* interested in the way a businessman conducts his business, the nightwatchman makes his rounds, the stenographer writes her letters, and He is pleased when work is done "heartily," enthusiastically.

The Lord *is* present when we make out our tax returns and expense accounts, and expects us to be fair and honest. He *is* concerned with the spirit in which we take our disappointments and successes, and how we stand up under prosperity and adversity. And if the work, the career, the activity, because of its nature cannot be dedicated to Him and performed conscientiously and enthusiastically, He does not want us to undertake it at all, and is displeased if we do.

Will religion and business mix? Yes, if it is the right kind of religion and the right kind of business. A business of such a character that it will not stand any admixture of Christian idealism is a business to be afraid of and shunned. Also, a religion that will not mix with and influence a man's business is no religion at all. It's dead and needs burying.

I submit that Christianity is supposed to be a living thing, a way of life, a Person-to-person and a person-to-Person relationship which gives a man an entirely new set of attitudes, purposes and motives, in business as well as in all other areas of life.

CHAPTER
2

THE PRIVILEGE of BEING a SERVANT

EVERYONE WHO WORKS HAS ONE OF TWO attitudes toward his job. Either he regards it merely and solely as a chance to get as much pay for himself as possible, or he regards it as an opportunity to serve other people, as well as himself. Among the first group are the shirkers, the loafers, the clock-watchers and all other types of poor and mediocre performers. Among the second group are the enthusiastic and inspired—the top performers.

Consider schoolteachers. We can all remember two or three schoolteachers who, whether we appreciated them or not when we were pupils in their classes, now hold an almost hallowed place in our memories by reason of their devotion to the difficult task of pounding knowledge into our inhospitable noggins. To illustrate, I know of a teacher of Latin in a girls' school, formerly attended by my daughters and granddaughter, who is so enthusiastic about the beauty of Latin conjugations and declensions and about the charm of Virgil's onomatopoeia, and who is so successful in transferring her enthusiasm to the minds and souls of her teen-age students that she has become a tradition among two generations of alumnae—a very live representative of a so-called dead language. She and her students give a banquet once a year, in which the honor students recline at the *mensa summa*. The parents also attend, dressed in Roman togas; and some of the fathers, as Senators, deliver speeches on which they have lavished much thought and preparation. Freshmen, dressed in the brown garb of slaves, wait on the tables. For a girl to be recognized with honors at this annual Latin banquet is almost as exciting as it would be for a high-school boy to make the state all-star football team. Miss Marguerite Grow, of The Hockaday School of Dallas, the remarkable woman who is responsible for all this enthusiasm for the Latin language, is of course no mere routine teacher. She is an inspired performer, an artist, and a *servant;* serving her students, her school, her profession and her beloved classics.

Consider clergymen. Some clergymen give the impression of being more interested in a comfortable and pleasant manner of living, with due public recognition of their wisdom and eloquence, than in their principal business which is to make individual men and women acquainted with Jesus Christ as Saviour, Lord and Friend. On the other hand, we all know of ministers and missionaries whose very lives, like St. Paul's, cry out: "For me to live is Christ!" These men are dedicated to the service of the Lord and human beings. Not concerned about salary, indifferent to pulpit popularity, they proclaim the gospel with authority and power. They spend much time with God, and by prayer and diligent study of the Scriptures, seek His will for every hour and every day of their lives. They walk with God and they also walk with men, striving always to bring them to Him in a vital, intimate relationship. These true ministers of the

gospel have attained the heights: they are *servants*.
Consider doctors. To some doctors, the sick person
is just another case to be processed through the mill as
rapidly as possible in order to make room for other
sick men to follow. While the patient's body is receiving highly technical treatment, his pocketbook is
undergoing equally expert analysis, and the final bill
that is presented to him, or to his widow, is likely to
be all that he or his estate can bear. On the other
hand, there are doctors by the thousands, both general practitioners and specialists, of whom it can be
said as it was said of the Great Physician Himself:
they "went about doing good." Such doctors, no matter how busy they may be or how specialized their
practice, take time to treat each patient with genuine
interest and personal concern. Many of their grateful patients can say something like this: "Thanks to
Dr. So-and-so, I am alive today. My case required
not only medical skill, but very close attention as
well, especially during the hours of crisis. He gave
me that kind of attention and pulled me through.
He's a great doctor and a great Christian. It is almost
worth the inconvenience and suffering of a severe
illness to fall into the hands of such a man. God bless
Dr. So-and-so!" Yes, may God indeed bless all such
doctors! They are true *servants*.

Consider businessmen. Some businessmen are
so intent upon the acquisition of personal wealth,
power and prestige, that they do not care whom they
hurt, or how many, in their climb to "success." In
fact, men of this kind sometimes deliberately hurt or
ruin others in order to help themselves. These are
the grabbers, the pushers, the shovers, the cold-
blooded rascals.

On the other hand, there are businessmen, and we all know many, who apparently take delight in using their money and their talents for the assistance and welfare of other people. Such men can do much good, and do.

All right-thinking businessmen realize that anyone connected with the management of a business is just a servant anyway. He is a servant of the owners of the business, a servant of the customers, a servant of the employees, a servant of the community, a servant of the local governments, a servant of Uncle Sam, a servant of many other people—and if he has the vision to see it and the courage to act upon it, a servant of God. Let the business executive realize that it is his function to serve; that's what he is there for and what he is paid for. Accordingly, let him strive to be a deserving, dedicated and efficient *servant*.

Consider *all* people who work, whether in stores, in factories, in offices, or in any other place of employment. Here again as we look at workers in general, we see on the one hand the self-centered, the loafers and the deadbeats, getting all they can and producing as little as possible; and on the other hand, those who conscientiously strive to be a good investment. In the company for which I work, the investment per employee is about $10,000. In another company in my city, the investment per employee is more than $70,000. This means that people somewhere—maybe our own neighbors—have invested a part of their savings in order to provide jobs for us. All of us who work should be grateful to those who put up the money to make our work possible. Our gratitude should express itself in an honest, intelligent and diligent effort to produce for them a good return on their investment in us. We should strive to be *servants*—good and faithful servants.

Consider Mrs. Alice Smothers. Thirty-four years ago she and her husband, J. W. Smothers, came to Malakoff, Texas, and followed a narrow clay road through the woods to a dingy, unsanitary shack known as the St. Paul School. J. W. Smothers, born of a slave father, had graduated from the Hampton Institute in Virginia with a B. S. degree in agriculture. Alice was a graduate of the Tuskegee Institute, of which her father, a minister, had been a trustee.

The husband-wife team had come to Malakoff to dedicate their lives to the service of their people. But what they saw when they arrived at the schoolhouse was so dismal that keen disappointment smote their souls. They knelt together and asked for God's strength and guidance. Then, they got up and got busy, cleaning and painting the old shack. The following year, with the aid of the Rosenwald Fund, they built a campus home and set up grades one to six. They let it be known that attendance was free to any Negro child, and in the fall of 1927 they took into their home five ragged little girls.

During those first years Alice and her husband cut the wood for cooking and heating. They toted all their drinking water in buckets for two miles. They took the children to the creek for bathing, and every week drove by wagon to Payne Springs to wash their clothes.

The Smotherses arranged for a bank loan to build an eight-room dormitory to house twenty-five children. As security for the loan, they pledged $150 per month out of their teachers' salary of $175. This left $25 per month for food and other operating expenses.

Agriculturist Smothers, whose two-acre garden soon was bursting with a variety of vegetables, raised more food than they could eat in one spring and summer. They borrowed pressure cookers and canned food for the winter months. Canning was added to the curriculum; this brought in a little money and much good publicity for the school. They taught the children how to pick cotton, and one summer the student body earned $500 in this way. They purchased a 2000-egg incubator for $150, the terms being $5 down and $5 per month.

In the years that have followed, the St. Paul Industrial Training School has grown, until today there are about 150 students. Most of these Negro boys and girls are the innocent victims of divorce, death, poverty or crime, and had no one to love them or even to care what became of them. Quite recently, eleven children, aged from nine months to fourteen years, who had been abandoned by their father and then made completely homeless by the death of their mother, were brought to St. Paul's and there found love and sympathy for their souls and abundant nourishment for their bodies.

Alice Smothers has made many friends among the white people of Dallas, Houston, and other Texas cities. Men and women of means have been so impressed with her heroism and unselfish devotion and the astonishing results of her ministry as expressed in the changed lives of Negro boys and girls, that cheerfully and eagerly they have opened up their pocketbooks to her. Alice recently called on a prominent philanthropist in Dallas to lay before him the need of the school for dairy cows. "Who sent you to me?" the philanthropist asked. "The Lawd sent me," replied Mrs. Smothers. Deeply impressed, the good man arranged immediately for a gift of twelve pedigreed cows.

On another occasion, Alice called on a prominent lady in Houston and told her story. When asked what she needed, Alice replied, "This morning I prayed that the Lawd would send me $1000 for today, but it's now six o'clock." The lady gave her a check for $1000, then and there. But that was not all. Later, when the lady learned how one of the city's delinquent Negro girls, having previously been picked up by the police many times, had developed under the Smotherses' influence into a fine Christian and one of the best cooks on the campus, she decided that a work which, through loving attention, made good citizens out of delinquents deserved her enthusiastic support. She gave $65,000 for the erection of a much-needed building and other facilities.

Now St. Paul's has 200 acres of land and total assets valued at $500,000, all free of debt. There are twelve teachers and five helpers. Funds are badly needed for a gymnasium, a chapel and another boys' dormitory. "The Lawd" will provide, because Alice Smothers and her husband will pray earnestly as though it all depended upon God, and then they will get out and work as though it all depended upon them. Friends, inspired by their sacrificial efforts, will take a keen pleasure in making their contributions and the work will go on, ever expanding.

Alice and J. W. Smothers are true *servants*.

When you stop to think about it, there is no higher calling on earth than to be a servant. The great leaders of men in all fields have not been the arrogant and the greedy, but the servants. The real servants are the true nobility. The greatest of all, the Son of God Himself, declared that He had come not to be served but to be a servant, and "to give his life a ransom for many." He said: "And whosoever will be chief among you, let him be your servant."

Paul liked to refer to himself as "Paul, a servant of Jesus Christ, called to be an apostle." Mrs. Alice Smothers considers herself to be a "servant of Jesus Christ, called to be a mother to 150 Negro children." A Christian manufacturer should regard himself as a "servant of Jesus Christ, called to be a manufacturer." A Christian stenographer should regard herself as "a servant of Jesus Christ, called to be a stenographer." There is no higher honor than to be a servant of Jesus Christ and of our fellow men.

CHAPTER
3

PROFITS and PEOPLE

PROBABLY EVERY DECISION THAT A BUSInessman has to make, and making decisions is his business, involves people and money. The executive is constantly faced with problems and dilemmas and, to quote Dr. Louis William Norris,[1] ". . . his principal problems are what he does about people . . . he is daily putting into action plans for people to carry out which in turn affect other people."

People and money. After all, what is business if not the art and science of making money with, by and for *people?*

I believe that there are three principal criteria by which an executive may judge his fitness for the job:

1. Do he and his associates make a profit for the company?
2. Are the profits earned fairly and honorably?
3. Are the profits dispensed or invested with justice and wisdom?

1. Does he make a profit for the company?

In American business, no matter how gentlemanly or noble an executive may be, the final judgment pronounced upon him by his peers is to be found in the last line of his company's operating statement: "Net profits after taxes." As a manager, he is not ". . .

[1] *Harvard Business Review*, Sept.-Oct. 1960.

the prime minister hired to preside over the dissolution of his majesty's empire. Even if he and his family own the company, he must succeed in the competitive whirl, or there will be no company over which he may reign as executive."[2]

No, the issue cannot be avoided. A manager, unless his company is under the umbrella of a government subsidy, must make a profit consistently, year after year. That's what they hired him for.

In the first place, his company's existence depends upon the executive's ability to operate it at a profit. Without profits, there can be no expansion in *good* times and no reserves to act like a blood bank in *bad* times to keep the enterprise alive. Without profits there cannot for long be credit, for no banker will lend money to a firm that cannot make money, and no supplier will sell on credit to a firm that has no credit. No profits can only mean no growth, no reserves, no credit, and therefore eventually no company.

In the second place, profitable operations are necessary not only that the enterprise may stay alive, but also for the sake of the general welfare of many people. In the previous chapter we had much to say about the manager of a company as a servant. We said that he is a servant of the stockholders, the customers, the employees, the government and the community. But how can he serve these various groups without profits? For example, how can he serve the community without profits? How can his company contribute its share to the Community Chest, the Red Cross, the hospitals, the colleges and all other worthwhile causes, without profits?

[2] *Ibid.*

And how can a company serve the government without profits? A corporation without income pays no income tax. Therefore, a corporation that fails to make a profit not only fails to carry its share of the cost of government, but also places upon the shoulders of other taxpayers the load it should be carrying itself. For what Uncle Sam requires, he will collect from someone—if necessary, from our grandchildren.

And how can a company serve its employees without profits? Pay raises, bonuses, retirement plans, vacations, holidays, coffee breaks, sick leave, hospitalization costs, group life insurance, unemployment insurance, workmen's compensation insurance, severance pay, and all other fringe benefits must be financed out of profitable operations. Obviously, if a company continuously loses money, it will be unable to provide fringe benefits. It will even be unable to provide full employment. Indeed, without profits, there will eventually be no jobs at all. It was a perceptive labor union leader who once said: "The greatest enemy of the working man is the company that fails to operate at a profit."

In fact, the company that fails to operate at a profit is practically everybody's enemy. No matter how kind and how benevolent its purposes may be, without profits it lacks the means of effecting those purposes.

It must be admitted, therefore—although reluctantly—that the first moral requirement of an American entrepreneur is to operate his enterprise at a profit. This is not always easy to do, as the break-even point constantly climbs, due to increasing costs and ever cheaper money; as competition, both domestic and foreign, grows continually more intense; as the tax load gets heavier and heavier; as labor unions demand and obtain higher and higher wages and more and more benefits, even though there is often no corresponding increase in the workers' productivity. But regardless of the difficulties involved, the executive must consistently produce profits if his company is to be healthy and growing, and a good corporate citizen.

Let me say at this point that while this chapter seems to be concerned with the chief executive of an enterprise, or at least with those executives who are on the "decision-making level," all that I have said so far has its application to every employee of the company. Each employee in an American enterprise is, in the last analysis, a member of the management team. He too must make important decisions. And while his decisions may not involve as much money, they do involve as many people as those made by the general manager. A blunder in judgment by the general manager may cost the company hundreds of thousands of dollars, while a blunder by a porter would not ordinarily involve more than a few dollars. Yet in both cases the same people are affected adversely—namely, the other employees, the customers, the stockholders—everyone who benefits when a company makes a profit and is hurt when it does not.

2. Are the profits earned fairly and honorably?

Profits should come as a reward for providing commodities or services that are beneficial to the man who buys them. On the other hand, if profits are the result of clever financial manipulations calculated to hurt someone else, the executives involved, no matter how "successful" they may be, should meet with the contemptuous disapproval of the public.

3. Are the profits dispensed or invested with justice and wisdom?

It is in the area of this third criterion that the executive copes with some of his most interesting problems and dilemmas. Each of the groups of people he serves desires a king-size share of the company's profits. Stockholders want dividends and, also, annual additions to surplus so that their stock may consistently increase in value. Employees want higher wages, shorter working hours, improved working conditions, greater fringe benefits. Customers want improved products and more and better service. The community wants contributions for worthy causes. The various governments want and of course obtain *their* share, in the form of taxes, excises, fees.

Since there are never enough dollars for everybody to be satisfied with the distribution, the executive must weigh one group against another, and as the judge of last resort, strike some sort of balance between them. He must exercise care not to be biased too much in favor of the closest and most clamant groups. For example, while listening to the demands of a labor union leader, he must also keep in mind the just needs of more distant and less vocal groups, such as his customers and stockholders.

What are some of the moral decisions that a business executive must make? Out of thousands of problems that come up in a small manufacturing business such as that with which I am connected, let me name only a very few. These are given merely as random examples.

Is it wise to hire handicapped people? In our company we employ two blind men, a man with multiple sclerosis and a few amputees. We find that, while these men cannot ordinarily work as fast as a normal employee, they usually make up for their handicaps by their enthusiasm and faithfulness. They value their jobs highly, and are never absent without good cause; they are seldom tardy. They make excellent citizens. One of our blind men, during the eighteen years he has been with us, has supported his wife and two children, paid for his home, purchased stock in the company, and is now putting his oldest child through college. The company policy of having several handicapped people seems to be working out all right in our case.

Is it wise to hire relatives? In our company, we go on the theory that if one member of a family is of good character and does outstanding work, the odds favor other members of the same family. As a result, we have many related folks on our payrolls—fathers, sons, grandsons, brothers, wives, sisters and daughters. Some employers would say that this is not a good policy.

Should we enforce retirement at age sixty-five when the retirement benefits normally begin? We don't have the courage to do this. After a man has been with us for thirty years or more, his job has become a vital part of his existence and to make him quit at age sixty-five might actually shorten his life. For example, consider the case of Daddy Jackmon, who remained on the job for fifteen years past the usual retirement age. Daddy operated a drill press and although his motions were slow, he kept on working all day long, almost never leaving his machine. The result was that at the end of the day he had turned out about as much work as an eighteen-year-old youngster would have done. One evening, Daddy

Jackmon, then seventy-nine, collapsed as he was leaving the plant upon completion of his day's work. I chanced to be nearby when it happened, and helped lift his frail body into a car. He was still alive when we got him home, but we felt certain that Daddy's working days were over. We were wrong. After a week of rest, he was back on the job and lasted more than a year before he finally gave up and died, a little past his eightieth birthday. Is it a mistake to keep a man past age sixty-five? Is it fair to the younger men in the organization?

In my company we have a few employees who seem to possess a real talent for getting into trouble. And it takes a good deal of someone's time, on the executive level, to help them out of trouble. Is it worth all this effort? I am thinking af a man I shall call Chance, whom my company many years ago financed in the purchase of a home. The purchase was covered by a contract of sale providing for interest at 3 per cent and small weekly installments to be deducted from the pay checks—no down payment. The only requirement in the contract was that Chance, while paying for his home, must do without an automobile.

This provision led to his downfall. Chance's wife wanted an automobile. She kept putting the pressure on him to buy a car until finally Chance decided, when his family was out of the city visiting relatives, that he would solve his problem by burning down the house. About two o'clock in the morning he threw together a pile of oil-soaked rags in the center of the living-room floor. Then, sitting on his bed in the neighboring room, he tossed a lighted match through the door toward the rags, leaving the decision to "fate." His marksmanship was good and almost immediately the house was on fire. To make sure that it burned down before the fire department could reach it, he started a number of other fires in various parts of the house. Unfortunately for him, the fire department arrived on the scene too promptly, before the various fires could get together.

A few hours later, Chance called me on the telephone to say that he was in jail charged with arson. Would I come down and help him? We talked to the fire marshal and other officials. Chance made a confession of his guilt and was promptly given a two-year suspended sentence. We then built his house back with the proceeds of the fire insurance, which had been taken out in our name, not his. With the approval of his fellow workers, Chance was reinstated in his job, and immediately took up his weekly payments where he had left off. In fact, he made two payments each week, one to us on the rebuilt house and the other directly to the insurance company on the house he had burned down.

After three or four years, real estate values in Chance's neighborhood went up spectacularly and he was able to sell his property for a great deal more than he had paid for it. As a result, the insurance company was completely reimbursed, the Mitchell Company was paid off in full, and Chance himself realized a nice profit over and above his equity. And he and his wife finally were able to have an automobile!

All this involved a lot of time and trouble. Is it a mistake for a small manufacturer to be concerned in the personal problems of an employee? Is this kind of paternalism wise, or is it foolish?

What about contributions? How far should a company go in making contributions? This is a real problem, even for a small company. I would estimate that the requests made upon us along this line would average at least two a day. If we were to make donations to all the causes for which we are solicited, and were to give each one as much as the solicitor wants us to give, our total annual contributions could easily eliminate our operating profits. All managers want their companies to be good corporate citizens. But they must also think about the interests of their stockholders and others whom they serve.

What about donations that are requested by valued customers for their own pet projects?

What about the question of short-range values versus long-range values? This problem comes up almost daily. How far should management go in the matter of paying out profits in dividends, bonuses, and so forth versus building up reserves for such areas as research and plant improvements?

These are just a few random examples of thousands of problems and dilemmas that an executive is called upon to face up to. Almost all of these problems and dilemmas involve, in one way or another, *people*. What help is available to a businessman in making his important decisions? This will be discussed in the next chapter.

CHAPTER
4

HELP for the
BUSINESSMAN

WHAT RESOURCES CAN A BUSINESSMAN call on for counsel and guidance in making important decisions affecting the welfare of so many people? Where can he look for help?

1. In the first place, he can consult his own experience. Stored up in his memory and in his files are thousands of precedents. These represent past decisions: some good with beneficial results, others bad with harmful, even disastrous, results. But whether good or bad, they are equally valuable—the one kind serving as a model to be tried again, the other as a bell buoy to warn against lurking rocks and dangerous shoals which have caused trouble before.

2. The executive not only draws upon his own experience, but also makes use of the experience and advice of others—of associates, staff members and consultants. There are available many experts to help him. In fact, every worker is "expert" in some particular or other and has ideas, which if there were time and opportunity to discover them, would be of much value to the executives of the company.

One means we use in my own company to tap some of these ideas of our employees is an Employees' Advisory Committee. This committee is composed of fifteen members, twelve of whom are factory employees chosen annually in a company-wide election, and three are representatives of management, including the company's president. The committee meets once each month in the Directors' Board Room. Its chairman is one of the employee members and serves for a term of one year. Not primarily a decision-making body, the committee is rather a discussion and advisory group. Any matter deemed by the chairman to be of general interest and affecting the general welfare may be brought up and freely discussed. All meetings are opened and closed with prayer, led by one of the members. With God's guidance and blessing thus invoked, and with the resulting fine spirit of cooperation, the success of the meetings is of course assured.

Such a committee may or may not be feasible for larger corporations, but I can heartily testify to its value in a small company like ours with its four hundred employees. It engenders a spirit of mutual understanding and enthusiastic teamwork; it also makes available ideas and attitudes which often can be utilized by management for the common good of the enterprise.

Numerous and various are the means at the executive's disposal for tapping the experience of other people. To mention only a few, there are: the business, trade and service organizations (our company belongs to sixty-four of them); the trade and technical periodicals (our company receives regularly 140 such periodicals); and professional consultants—specialists in their respective fields (our company pays for the part-time services of nineteen such specialists, besides benefiting from the help of numerous other experts on the payroll of our suppliers, our customers, various governmental agencies, and others).

3. Another force which exerts a powerful influence on the decisions of executives is the thousands of laws and regulations pertaining to business operations. Such laws are particularly effective with men who are inclined to be unscrupulous. With a man whose chief motive for being "good" is the threat of severe punishment for being "bad," there is naturally nothing more influential than a law with teeth in it. In fact, it was the piratical activities of rascals like Commodore Vanderbilt, Daniel Drew, Jay Gould and Jim Fiske that brought into being much of this restrictive legislation.

Now, two or three generations later, the laws, necessary though they are, have become so numerous and their ramifications have become so complex that the average businessman, no matter how good his intentions, cannot possibly keep up with all of them. In fact, he can no longer look for legal advice to one corporation lawyer; instead, he must hire a number of legal specialists—one for tax law, another for laws against price discrimination, another for patent laws, still another for anti-trust laws, and so forth.

One boy in Holland saved his country from inundation by holding his thumb in a hole in the dike. But had there been a million holes requiring a million thumbs, the situation would have been confusing, to say the least. So with a million laws and regulations; the results for a businessman are indeed confusing, often bewildering, and sometimes painful.

A case in point is my own experience with the Walsh-Healy Act. I hardly knew that there was such a law until one day I learned from a federal inspector that we were in violation of one of its provisions. The inspector had spent almost two weeks in our plant inquiring of every employee about our hiring procedures, working rules, wage rates, and personnel practices.

In his interview with me which followed, the inspector told me affably between puffs on his pipe that our working conditions were fine, our employee morale was excellent, and, as to our compliance with the law, everything was in "apple-pie order"—except for one item. But this item was serious. We were permitting our people in the Navy Rocket Division to take two ten-minute coffee breaks each day, one in the morning and one in the afternoon, *on their own time*. This, he said, was a violation. I quickly pointed out that the employees themselves, three or four years previously, had voted unanimously in favor of changing the coffee breaks from company expense to their own expense, in consideration of a general pay increase of ten cents per hour. The inspector replied that any agreement between employer and employees to violate the law, even if made in ignorance of the violation, was itself illegal. He said that we would have been in the clear had the rest periods been twenty minutes long instead of ten minutes; that a departmental regulation interpreting the law had set twenty minutes as the minimum which could be allowed for a rest period at employees' expense. Anything less than twenty minutes must be at company expense. In other words, if our company had provided only one coffee break twenty minutes long instead of two coffee breaks of ten minutes each, we would have been within the law. The theory, the inspector said, was that a twenty-minute period gave an employee sufficient time to transact personal business, whereas a ten-minute period did not. I argued the point at some length but did not get anywhere. The inspector, who was a likable chap, informed me that he could not personally change the law or the regulations, that his duty was to report the violation and then let his superiors fight it out with us—in court. "And, by the way," he added ominously, "the department has a staff of lawyers who do not appear to be very busy right now and I have an idea that they would welcome a test case on this issue."

Well, our company *was* very busy then and we had no desire to spend a lot of time and money in the courts. So we decided at once to reinstate our former practice of providing the rest periods on company time, at company expense. Then came the real blow. The inspector told us gently that the law would have to be applied retroactively to the preceding two years. He stated that we had the option of paying the employees the amounts that had been "earned" during these two rest periods each day for the past two years, or of paying the entire amount—about $70,000—to the government.

We referred the matter to our lawyers. Their opinion was that if we were to appeal the decision of the Wage and Hour Division, we would probably win in the lower courts but would lose in the Supreme Court. Meanwhile, the management had argued themselves into the conviction that it would be a good thing to make the payments, anyway. After all, the employees had done a magnificent job during the war years. They had won the Army-Navy E five times. They deserved this windfall bonus. Besides, Uncle Sam would stand more than half the cost because the

company was in the 52 per cent income-tax bracket for
the years involved.

Accordingly, we called a meeting of the employees
and told them the whole story. To my surprise, many
of them disapproved and were in fact indignant about
the inspector's findings. One man jumped up and declared that he would not take his portion of more
than $400. He said he needed the money but it wasn't
fair to require the company to pay it. He remembered
distinctly that the whole matter had been settled and
unanimously agreed to by a company-wide election
held three or four years previously. Several others
rose to make similar statements. Soon the spokesman
for management was arguing with the employees *for*
a position he had been arguing *against* with the inspector. The clincher that ended the debate was the
assurance we gave the employees that if they did not
accept the settlement, the $70,000 would still have to
be paid anyway, but to the government as a penalty.
So the matter was settled to the mutual satisfaction
of company and employees, and the inspector, judging by his genial attitude, seemed to be well pleased
also.

But isn't it too bad that men need so many laws?

And isn't it too bad that the legal technology of
business has to be so involved? Consider, for example, the instructions that accompany our federal
income tax declaration, Form 1040-ES. As a mental
exercise, try after one reading to put the substance of
this clause in your own words:

10. Additional Charge for Failure To Pay Estimated
Income Tax.—The following additional charge is im-
posed by law for underpayment of any installment of
estimated tax: 6 percent per year for the period of the

underpayment on the difference between the installment payment made and 70 percent (66⅔ percent in the case of farmers) of the installment due on the basis of the final return or tax for the year.

The charge with respect to any underpayment of any installment is mandatory and will be made unless the total amount of all payments of estimated tax made on or before the last date prescribed for the payment of such installment equals or exceeds whichever of the following is the lesser—

(a) The amount which would have been required to be paid on or before such date if the estimated tax were whichever of the following is the least—

(1) The tax shown on your return for the previous year (if your return for such year showed a liability for tax and covered a taxable year of 12 months), or

(2) A tax computed by using the previous year's income with the current year's rates and exemptions, or

(3) 70 percent (66⅔ percent in the case of farmers) of a tax computed by projecting to the end of the year the income received from the beginning of the year up to the beginning of the month of the installment payment; OR

(b) An amount equal to 90 percent of the tax computed, at the rates applicable to the taxable year, on the basis of the actual taxable income for the months in the taxable year ending before the month in which the installment is required to be paid.

The American executive, in addition to his other duties and burdens, must keep informed the best he can as to all the laws and regulations pertaining to his business. He must play the game according to the rules laid down for him. And he should do it cheerfully and wholeheartedly—like a good sport.

As a matter of fact, we businessmen in the United States enjoy more freedom and more privileges of the right kind than perhaps any other businessmen in the world. We still have a good economic climate in which to work. We still have the best government in existence today. We should be willing to keep it so by serving it, by fighting for it, and certainly by a scrupulous observance of its laws.

We who have been entrusted with places of importance in business should frequently go to our knees before God and thank Him that we are *American* businessmen.

That is truly something to be grateful for.

4. Finally, there is Divine guidance. If we believe in a personal God, why not turn to Him and to His word for correction, encouragement, wisdom and guidance? Of course, if our God is a depersonalized abstraction of the kind described by a distinguished educator as "that interaction between individuals, groups and agencies, which generates and promotes the greatest mutuality of good," there is no use in taking up our problems with him—or it. Who can expect help, inspiration or guidance from an interaction?

The same God whom David addresses as his Shepherd in that most beautiful of all poems, the Twenty-third Psalm, is the God of the Apostle Paul, of Augustine, of the Christian heroes and martyrs of all ages, of George Washington and Abraham Lincoln, of sailors adrift on a life raft, of scared doughboys in their foxholes—and should be the God of the businessman, as well. *They* prayed to Him: so should he. *They* put their trust in Him: so should he. *They* sought to please Him and to honor His name: so should he.

The God of the Bible is not some aloof, disinterested Force; He is a Person who, although infinite, eternal, and the Creator of all things, is yet intimately acquainted with us as individuals. He takes note of our every act and is fully cognizant of the words we speak and of the thoughts we think. The God of the Bible is concerned about the eternal welfare of all men. The supreme proof of this is what He did two thousand years ago; He projected Himself into human history and became a man Himself and lived among us—"the image of the invisible God." And they called His name Jesus, which means Saviour.

And Jesus went about performing acts of compassion, speaking marvelous and amazing words.

He made astonishing claims and promises. "I and my Father are one," He declared, ". . . he that hath seen me hath seen the Father . . . no man cometh unto the Father, but by me. . . . He that heareth my word, and believeth on him that sent me, hath everlasting life. . . . The Son of man came not to be ministered unto [served], but to minister [serve], and to give his life a ransom for many. . . . I am the good shepherd: the good shepherd giveth his life for the sheep. . . . he that believeth in me, though he were dead, yet shall he live" (John 10:30; John 14:9; John 14:6; John 5:24; Matthew 20:28; John 10:11; John 11:25).

Jesus' ministry lasted only three or four years, but during that brief period He accomplished, by His life, death and resurrection, infinitely more for mankind than have all other lives put together. Although He wrote no autobiography, no books, the words He spoke are eternal; as He said, "Heaven and earth shall pass away, but my words shall not pass away" (Matthew 24:35). And they have not.

Such claims as Jesus made are either true or false. If false, then we are forced to say that Jesus was no good man at all, but either an imposter or a lunatic. On the other hand, if the claims are true, then we must say that He is God. A Christian is simply one who, believing Christ's assertions to be true, has accepted Him as divine Saviour, and has crowned Him as King in his heart.

Now, it seems to me that the only alternative to yielding our hearts to God is to remain on the throne ourselves. Either we take Christ for our King or we follow the philosophy which asserts: "I am the master of my fate. I am the captain of my soul." Plain common sense tells us that such a philosophy is pompous drivel. No man can control his future—not even the next five minutes of it. Even while he is boasting, some sub-microscopic, unnamed, unknown bug may be at work on him, to take him to physical death and to the dissolution of his body. Then where will the captain be? Where then will be the master of his fate?

Even while I was putting down the words of the preceding paragraph, the time being six o'clock in the morning, my phone rang to bring the news that Jim Brawley was dead. We had thought that Jim was well on the road to recovery following an operation for cancer. But during the night a crisis had come unexpectedly, and our dear friend was no longer with us. Jim was not one to fool around with this "I-am-the-master-of-my-fate" nonsense. Years ago, he had accepted Christ as his Saviour and as *the* Master of his life. There was nothing dramatic about Jim, but in his quiet way, he let it be known that his allegiance was to Christ. The folks in the Traffic Department knew it, and so did all the rail-

road and truck line people who called on him, as
Traffic Manager. His life spoke out for Him. With
the Apostle Paul, Jim could say: "I know whom I
have believed, and am persuaded that he is able to
keep that which I have committed unto him against
that day" (II Timothy 1:12). That day, for Jim,
had arrived, and it was a day of triumph.

As for me, I claim the same Lord and Saviour. I
find Him adequate for every need of my life.

What has all this to do with business? Merely this:
If He is our Lord and personal Friend, we will want
to share with Him our programs, our ambitions, our
problems, our disappointments, our progress.

If the Christian in business has the courage to let
Christ rule in his life, saying in his own heart: "As
for me and my company, we will serve the Lord,"
then his vocation will take on a new meaning, a new
assurance, a new excitement, a new joy.

Mysterious? Yes, but highly practical, as well.

Does God's presence with us in our business, does
our faith in Him, guarantee financial success? This
will be discussed in the next chapter.

CHAPTER
5

DOES FAITH in GOD INSURE SUCCESS in BUSINESS?

ONE DAY IN 1947, THE PURCHASING Agent of our company came into my office with a problem. He held in his hand a screw about three fourths of an inch long. It was little, but it was important. We were using several hundred of these special, patented screws in every cotton cleaning machine we manufactured, and normally ordered them in lots of a million or more at a time. There was no substitute for this screw, and there was only one source of supply, a New York concern which I shall call the Klein Manufacturing Company.

Now, instead of the usual six months' supply, our stock had dwindled to a scant two weeks' supply. The P. A. said that the Klein people were several months behind with their shipments on our orders. This was not their fault, he added, but was due to an acute steel shortage; they could not obtain the steel wire necessary for producing the screws.

And so our company faced the bleak prospect of a shutdown. For more than fifteen years we had not laid off, even for one day, a single regular full-time worker for lack of work. Now, that record was about to be ended by a general layoff which, if it should last long enough, would work a severe hardship on our employees. Furthermore, since the threatened shutdown would come just when we were approaching our peak production and shipping season, we would lose more than a million dollars of business that would be canceled by customers who could not wait.

The Purchasing Agent had worked hard on the problem. He had written many letters and had sent many telegrams; also, he had made several long distance telephone calls, finally putting the matter squarely up to the president, Mr. Klein, himself. Mr. Klein had written us: "We are sorry to say that it looks very much as though we will be unable to take care of you in accordance with your requirements. It is very distasteful for us to have to give you this information in view of the fact that you have been one of our loyal customers for the past fifteen years, but in this respect you are in no different position than several score of our other friends. Like yourselves, over the years we have been supplying such well-known concerns as Philco, RCA, Ford, Frigidaire, Pullman Standard Car, New York Central, General Electric, Westinghouse, and many other prominent manufacturers too numerous to mention. . . ."

When the P. A. left my office, I stared glumly at the little screw which he had left with me, wondering how so small a thing could cause so great a crisis.

Finally, and I am afraid it was a last, desperate resort, I decided to take the matter "upstairs" to the Chief Executive. In other words, I prayed to the Lord for guidance and help. The reader will judge for himself from the rest of this story to what extent the prayer was answered.

My reasoning, which I will readily admit was rather farfetched, went something like this. There must be *some* steel wire available—enough to produce *some* screws for *some* customers—and the Klein Company, if properly convinced of our dire need, would surely place us high on their priority list. Further, *somewhere* in New York City there must be *some* person who was preëminently qualified to present our cause to Mr. Klein. Who this person was, I had not the slightest idea. But it occurred to me as a rather forlorn hope that *some* New York banker could probably tell us how to proceed to find such a man. To locate such a banker was in itself a problem.

I decided to start with Mr. Milton Brown, President of the Mercantile National Bank in Dallas. Upon hearing our story, he suggested that we call the executive vice president of one of the largest banks in the world—a gentleman whom I shall refer to as Mr. Marshall. In ten minutes' time Mr. Marshall was on the phone. Then I began to feel how presumptuous it was for a little manufacturer deep in the heart of Texas to be bothering a great banker in New York City about so trivial a matter as a barrel of screws. However, I had gone too far to back out; and so, after due apologies, I told my story to Mr. Marshall. Could he by any chance help me find someone in New York City who could listen to my story and then relay the facts to Mr. Klein with such urgency and persuasiveness as to get some screws for us?

To my amazement, it then developed that Mr. Marshall, himself, was well acquainted with the Klein Manufacturing Company. He knew Mr. Klein personally. Mrs. Marshall and Mrs. Klein were good friends and, if I remember correctly all the facts at this late date, he even had some official capacity with the company. Furthermore, he had once been asked by another company, much larger than ours, to do what he could, to obtain some of the same kind of screws for them. At this point, I exclaimed, "Mr. Marshall, do you realize how remarkable this is? In ten minutes' time I have located on the telephone, over 1600 miles away, the one man among seven million people in New York City who can really help us. Were you successful in getting some screws for your other friends?"

"Yes, it so happens that I was able to help them out," replied Mr. Marshall, "and I shall, of course, be glad to do what I can for you and for my friends at the Mercantile Bank there in Dallas."

Two or three days after this conversation, we had a telegram from Mr. Klein indicating that he now understood from Mr. Marshall how urgent our need was; that fortunately his company had just received a small shipment of wire and they were giving our order special preference; that 100,000 screws would be shipped by air freight within a week, with other shipments to follow rapidly until our order was completed. His promise was kept to the letter; the screws arrived just in time. Not a single hour of production was lost. No one was laid off. No orders were canceled.

Immediately we proceeded to telephone Mr. Brown of the Mercantile Bank to thank him for his part in solving our problem. Then we wired Mr. Klein to thank him. We of course wrote a warm letter to Mr. Marshall expressing our gratitude to him. (Incidentally, we were greatly pleased a few weeks later to read that Mr. Marshall had become the president of his great bank.) Finally, we took the matter up with the One who had engineered it all, the Lord Himself, and said "thank you" to Him.

I realize that many people would regard the events I have just related as merely a chain of remarkable coincidences. Such folks would no doubt contemn the idea that God can be interested in anything so trivial as a nearly empty screw barrel. To think He *is* interested in such matters, they would say, is childlike and presumptuous.

What is wrong with being childlike? Does not God commend childlikeness in us—yes, demand it? Jesus says, "Suffer little children . . . to come unto me: for *of such* is the kingdom of heaven. . . . Except ye be converted; and become as *little children*, ye shall not enter into the kingdom of heaven" (Matthew 19:14; 18:3). And, "without faith it is impossible to please him: for he that cometh to God must believe that he is, and that he is a rewarder of them that diligently seek him" (Hebrews 11:6).

It seems to be the universal testimony of God's servants, both in the Bible and out of it, that He does hear and answer their prayers. Sometimes the answer is "Yes," sometimes "No," and sometimes it is "Wait a while." Doesn't an intelligent, loving father of today do the same thing with *his* son? Sometimes *he* says "Yes," sometimes "No," and sometimes *he* says, "Let's wait a while, son." Is God inferior to an earthly father in wisdom or in love? Then why not trust Him to know and do what is to our ultimate best interest? As sensible children of an all-wise Heavenly Father whom we love, because "He first loved us and gave himself for us," we should readily submit to His will, whether or not it coincides with our own desires.

Does faith in God guarantee success in business? Of course not. There are some kinds of business in which a Christian has no business at all. But assuming that a given business is one in which a Christian can engage with good conscience, will he be sure of success just because he is a Christian? Of course not.

To answer "Yes" would be to assume that God is under obligation to reward every Christian with money for every "good" thing he does. If such a philosophy prevailed, men would soon be near to bursting with "goodness," holding out their hands for the prize money and thanking God—and themselves—for being better than other men. Prigs of this kind would be both counterfeit Christians and sorry businessmen, in the bargain.

Surely no sincere Christian would regard God as a sort of glorified servant, like Aladdin's genie, ready whenever the lamp is rubbed to accede to his every whim.

The only bearing that real Christianity has on business success is to ask: How is this success being achieved? What is the man doing with it? Is the Lord Christ honored and served in the whole matter? How does His servant endure success? And how does His servant stand up under disappointment and failure? If, due to factors quite beyond his control, a Christain experiences some great disappointment or some serious setback in his business, how does he adjust to such a disappointment or setback? Does he accept the experience in good grace, thank God for it and rejoice in the knowledge that "all things work together for good to them that love God"? Will he tackle the new situation with courage, energy and enthusiasm, asking for guidance and wisdom that he may proceed in a way satisfying to the Lord?

It is possible, I think, for a Christian to be a successful failure. It is possible for him to deal with a financial failure in his business in such a way that the outcome will be a spiritual victory. I offer as an exhibit the story that my father used to tell, many years ago, about a plumber in St. Louis. This plumber and his partner, due to circumstances beyond their control, went broke. The bank, of which my father was a director, charged off about $15,000 when the bankruptcy settlement was made. In due course the bank officials forgot about the matter.

However, Mr. A, the plumber, did not forget. One day, about five years after the bankruptcy, he showed up at the bank and told the cashier that he wanted to pay $100 on his note. The cashier called in the president, who explained that Mr. A was under no legal obligation to make any further payments on the indebtedness. Mr. A knew that; yes, he also knew that so far as any moral obligation was concerned his former partner was as much involved as he. But regardless of all this, he wanted to pay off the whole debt himself and if the Lord favored him with good health and good business in his new enterprise, he would do it. And he did! It required three or four years to pay off the entire balance but toward the end the payments got bigger and closer together.

The bank's officers tried to persuade him to accept a portion of the debt as a "gift," but he would not hear of it. Finally, when the last payment was made and Mr. A left the bank with his note marked "Paid," he could know that he had indeed walked the second mile. No doubt he was pleased to reflect that the A

Plumbing Company was now a flourishing enterprise and enjoyed splendid prospects for future business. Certainly he had the assurance that all the people at the bank, and all their friends, would favor him with their plumbing business. But I like to imagine that to Mr. A the greatest satisfaction of all was to hear the Voice speaking quietly to his heart these words: "Well done, good and faithful servant: thou hast been faithful . . ." (Matthew 25:23).

What is success for a Christian businessman? As a *businessman,* the Christian must submit himself to judgment by the same standards that apply to all businessmen: Does he operate his business at a profit? But as a *Christian,* he must also submit himself to God's standards. He must walk humbly before his God, seeking on all occasions the Father's will, consulting Him in prayer, serving Him by being of service to other people, enduring hardships with valor and thankfulness, taking successes with gratitude but with humility and caution, giving Him the honor when things go well, and placing the blame upon himself, where it usually belongs, when things go wrong.

There could be no finer praise for a worker, whether a company executive or a man in coveralls, than the statement made concerning one of God's servants thousands of years ago: "And Enoch walked with God: and he was not; for God took him" (Genesis 5:24). Enoch's was an eternal success. That is the kind of success that God guarantees for each of us, if we want it earnestly enough to submit ourselves to His will.

CHAPTER
6

CAVEAT EMPTOR

WHAT IF RIP VAN WINKLE HAD SLEPT
for two hundred years instead of twenty? What if,
after awakening from his long nap, he had made his
slow descent in the Catskills, not during the peaceful
1780's, but in the clamorous, head-long 1960's? What
if he had returned to society in *our* generation?

What would Rip think if today for the first time he
should look down from the top of a hill upon the
highway traffic hurtling north to Albany and south
to New York City? Imagine his terror on beholding
for the first time a fourteen-wheel diesel transport—
as big as the farmhouse which he had shared with
Dame Van Winkle and the children—roaring past on
its way to the big city.

Suppose that, after his two-hundred-year sleep had
received its due publicity, and Rip had become
famous, he should go to the city, himself—perhaps to
be a guest on the Ed Sullivan Show, or to appear on
some other TV program in behalf of a brand of tooth
paste, breakfast cereal, or vitamin pills. What would
Rip think of the city?

What would he think of the crowds? In one minute
he would behold more people on the sidewalks of
New York than he had seen during his whole lifetime
at home. Surely he would look with wonder upon the
hordes streaming daily to and from their work. He
would notice how the masses of people go to and

from their daily activities in accordance with a common pattern of four great movements. First, in the morning, there is the horizontal, converging movement, as the people disgorge from their automobiles, taxis, buses, trains, subway cars and ferryboats and move along the sidewalks and across the streets into the central congested area. Then follows a vertical, upward movement, as they pack themselves into elevators and are whisked to their respective floors to take their appointed places in their appointed cubbyholes. A few hours later, there is a vertical downward movement as they return to the sidewalks and streets. And finally comes the great horizontal, centrifugal movement as they scramble for their automobiles and taxis, and for seats or standing room on buses, trains, subway cars and ferryboats and move out toward the periphery as fast as they can safely get away. Rip would surely wonder at these great movements of people each day. He would wonder why all this concentration, this amazing congestion in one small area.

Well, why *are* all these people here? Are they not here mostly to sell something to each other, to do business with each other and with people outside the city? Almost all of them have something to sell: either commodities, as the real estate brokers, shoe clerks and soda jerkers; or services, as the schoolteachers, baseball players and lawyers.

This is an era of selling. There never was in all the history of the world such a time for buying and selling as the present time, or such a place for it as a modern American city.

Our total expenditures in this country—individual, corporate and governmental—will in this year of 1962 exceed $500,000,000,000. This means an average of more than $2,500 for every man, woman and child in the United States. In other words, if all the people were taxpayers and each one had to bear his proportionate part of the expenditures of the federal, state and local *governments;* and if all the people were corporate stockholders and each one were assessed his share of the expenditures of *corporations;* and if all the people spent exactly the same amount on *themselves* for their own needs and desires, the share of total expenditures—governmental, corporate, and personal—for a family of five people would be $12,500.

Contrast Rip's buying activities in the eighteenth century with mine in the twentieth. He probably made only one or two purchases a week. His needs and his wants were simple; and such as they were, he and his wife were able to supply most of them by their own efforts. The farm provided their staple food. Rip's gun furnished most of the delicacies for their table. Dame Van Winkle made most of their clothing. Certainly they had little need for guilders or dollars, or for credit; he seldom had to buy anything, either for cash or "on terms." I, on the other hand, am constantly making purchases: newspapers, books, lunches, razor blades, tooth paste, electric current, water, gas, and a thousand other commodities and services.

When Mr. Van Winkle sat down to a meal at his table, most of his food had traveled only a few feet to reach his kitchen. On the other hand, when I ate lunch today—navy bean soup, a chicken sandwich and a glass of iced tea—many of the items had traveled hundreds of miles, and literally thousands of people had had a part in their production, transportation and preparation. When I paid for my simple meal at the cashier's desk, I was, in effect, consummating a purchase of at least twenty commodities: navy beans grown in Illinois, water from a lake thirty miles away, salt from East Texas, pepper from Java, bay leaves from India, chicken from southern Texas, milk and eggs from Dallas County, butter from Wisconsin, flour from wheat grown in Kansas and milled in Minnesota, olives from California, pickles from cucumbers grown in southern Texas, vinegar from Pennsylvania, tea from Ceylon, sugar from Louisiana and various herbs and condiments from various parts of the earth. All of these had been collected for my table by the genial proprietor who had also provided for my benefit the services of chefs, waitresses, bus boys, janitors, cashiers and bookkeepers.

A large part of my purchasing is impersonal. Often I do not see the people from whom I buy. I can dial a telephone number and be in immediate contact with a salesman, place my order and receive delivery within a few hours, and a bill within a few days. The check I mail in payment will set off a chain of reactions—mostly mechanical—in two or three banks and the clearing house, and the funds will be transferred from my account to that of the vendor, thus consummating a transaction in which I have met nobody face to face.

Especially impersonal is my purchase of gas, water and electricity. I merely push a button or turn a handle and immediately there becomes available a bountiful supply of water for a hundred different uses; or gas for heating my home and cooking my food; or electric power to keep my food cold and my electric blanket warm, to heat water and to freeze ice cubes, to turn fans and blowers; to operate dishwashers, vacuum cleaners, laundry machines, can openers and ice cream freezers; to banish the darkness with soft or brilliant lights; to turn on my gas furnace automatically, at a prescribed time or at a pre-set temperature; to put clocks to work telling the time; to ring door bells; and to furnish entertainment by means of TV, radio and records.

This system of metered vending has made it easy for all of us in America today to consume vast quantities of water, gas, electric current and other commodities. For example, the average family of five people in Dallas purchases and uses about 750 gallons of water per day. In Rip's time this would have meant about 187 trips to the spring each day with two two-gallon buckets.

Rip made his own candles. Assuming that each candle had a life of eight hours, I estimate that I consume 280 of Rip's candles every night in the form of electric current for lighting my home. Lamps in our yard are each equipped with a simple photoelectric relay which turns them on at dusk and off at dawn. I don't even work the switch—the sun does it for me. The current flows; a meter measures and registers the kilowatt-hours; an electronic computer makes out my bill.

Rip probably never heard of credit. The word "credit" which is so important a part of the modern business vocabulary was seldom used in his time. In fact, the phenomenal growth of credit purchasing is comparatively recent. Only fifty years ago, in financing the purchase of a home, the required down payment ordinarily was at least 50 per cent of the purchase price. In recent years, the required down payment percentage has become smaller and smaller until very soon, thanks to FHA, VA and the taxpayers of U.S.A., no down payment at all will be required in qualified cases. Furthermore, the installment payments are spread over a period of so many years that the loan is likely to outlive the purchaser, and the home itself.

Nowadays you can buy anything on credit. A young man borrows money for his education, his engagement ring, his honeymoon trip. He goes in debt for his babies, his home, his furniture, his automobile and his TV set. When, later in life, sickness overtakes him, he borrows money to pay the doctors, the ambulance, the hospital, the nurses; and finally when he dies, the family borrows money for his funeral and burial. The credit man is interested in him from the womb to the tomb.

All of us in this year of our Lord 1962 are engaged in selling to and buying from one another. Some of the commodities and services we buy and sell will last less than ten minutes; others will outlive our grandchildren. Look at the never-ending list: hair tonic, soap, detergents, face powder; golf balls, baseballs, footballs, basketballs, soccer balls, tennis balls, ping pong balls and marbles; guns, skis, fishing tackle, swim suits; pansies and live oak trees; gasoline, tires and spark plugs; paint for barns, for lips and eyelids, and for works of impressionistic art; a thousand things to drink, from buttermilk for plain people to whiskey for the "man of distinction"; trips to San Francisco, Paris, Hong Kong, Anchorage, Muleshoe in Texas, and Belleville in Illinois; battleships, missiles, space rockets, bombs and Bibles; also

—in sequence—diapers, bassinets, building blocks, high chairs, blue jeans, skates, bicycles, wrenches, screw drivers, letterheads, swivel chairs, Bermuda shorts, reducing pills, tranquilizers, wheel chairs, crutches, cemetery lots, tomb stones, and the services of lawyers to settle estate and inheritance taxes and to help resolve disputes among the beneficiaries.

In the series of contrasts between Rip Van Winkle's time and our own, we have tried to indicate some of the reasons for the astronomical expansion of buying and selling in America during the past century or two. Let us now list seven of these reasons as follows:

1. Modern specialized production methods resulting in greatly increased purchasing power for the average American.

2. The concurrent increase in leisure time caused by reducing our work week from seventy-two hours to forty hours.

3. The development of modern packaging methods and modern transportation facilities.

4. The birth and growth of modern methods of communication.

5. The development of modern banking methods and bookkeeping machinery.

6. The vast growth of credit facilities.

7. The development of metered vending.

These seven factors, I believe, account in a large measure for the frenzied tempo of buying and selling in America today.

But not altogether. One other factor must be added to the list, a strange, elusive factor that works with and through all the others. This factor is modern American salesmanship. What is it?

Salesmanship is the art of creating in another per-

son an impelling urge to buy what the vendor wants
to sell.

In order to create the urge to buy, the vendor
usually finds it expedient to appeal to some quality—
good, bad or indifferent—in the prospect's character:
laziness, fear, pride, snobbishness, ambition, love of
family, love of country, love of money, the desire of
men to be popular and of women to be beautiful and
charming, the wish to conform or the desire to be
different, or any one of a hundred other traits.

Rosser Reeves, the distinguished advertising man,
in his book *Reality in Advertising* says:

It is quite surprising how much we can find out about
what moves people. We can find out, within very practical limits, what people want in a given product; and
there is an incredibly long list of proved desires out of
which we can evolve a diversity of creative, and imagina-
tive, campaigns. We know, for example, that we do not
want to be fat. We do not want to smell bad. We want
healthy children, and we want to be healthy ourselves.
We want beautiful teeth. We want good clothes. We
want people to like us. We do not want to be ugly. We
seek love and affection. We want money. We like comfort. We yearn for more beautiful homes. We want
honesty, self-respect, a place in the community. We want
to own things in which we can take pride. We want to
succeed in our jobs. We want to be secure in our old age.

The list of proved desires can be expanded, page after
page; and here again you are staring at reality in advertising, for these are not gambles and speculations, but
the very stuff and substance out of which great campaigns are made.[1]

It is interesting to thumb through the pages of any

[1] Rosser Reeves, *Reality in Advertising* (New York, Alfred A.
Knopf, Inc.) .

periodical and to analyze the advertisements. Why does a certain advertisement appeal to us? What trait of character causes us to be interested in a particular advertisement? Does the advertisement create in us an urge to buy the product? If so, why?

Such a pastime may prove to be as much a self-analysis as an analysis of advertisements.

It is obvious that all of us respond in a greater or lesser measure to the pressures of salesmanship. If you believe that you are immune, just take an inventory of useless or downright harmful purchases you have made within the last year. Look at the books you have been enticed to buy but have never read and never will read. Consider the bric-a-brac and gimcracks you have put in your home to gather dust and to get in the way. Consider the money you have spent for "good times," whatever your definition of "good times" may be. Consider the salesmanship which beguiled you into purchasing a make of car completely out of your "class," or a trip around the world when you really could afford only a vacation in Wisconsin, or a trip to Miami when you could better afford taking the kids to Grandma's house in the next county.

The combination of salesmanship, on the one hand, and the extension of easy credit, on the other, have caused many people to plunge themselves hopelessly into debt for the purchase of items that they could easily have done without.

Not long ago one of the employees of our company came to me with a financial problem. He and his wife had succumbed to sales pressures and to the desire to keep up with some of their better-off neighbors, and had bought not only all of the "necessities" for housekeeping, but also many of the "luxuries." All of these purchases were made on easy, long-term credit.

Soon Lee was in arrears with all of his monthly installments. He had borrowed the limit from our Employees Loan Committee and, when sickness came with hospital and doctor bills, had gone to the loan sharks. By the time we found out about his situation, Lee was hopelessly in the clutches of nine such loan sharks. He had obligated himself to pay an exorbitant rate of interest, and also fees for drawing up the papers, life insurance premiums, and other charges.

Armed with a list of his debts, we spent about two hours on the telephone calling one after another of the loan sharks. In each case we offered to advance the necessary funds to pay the exact amount of the principal only, with no interest, no fees, no premiums, no penalties. We told each one of the lenders that he could either accept our offer or sue the employee. If he sued, the company lawyer would defend the suit, and the company lawyer, who at that time was president of the American Bar Association, would no doubt be interested in a thorough investigation of their usurious practices. All nine accepted our proposal and we paid them off.

Lee has learned his lesson. He knows now that he must stiffen his resistance to sales blandishments and easy credit; that he must keep his desire to own and enjoy things within his earning power to provide them.

Caveat emptor. Let the buyer beware, indeed. But not so much of the vendor as of himself, lest his desires to possess and enjoy outrun his capacity to buy and pay for.

The Christian especially should be cautious about his purchases. In our wonderfully properous America, it is very easy to buy too much and to overextend our credit. A Christian who makes someone else suffer because he fails to pay his bills and to take care of his pledges has a sorry testimony in the business world.

A Christian should also be careful about what he buys with his money. There are many things that he has no business purchasing at all. He will even want to deny himself some things that might be enjoyable or profitable for himself, in favor of other commodities and services that will be helpful to his family, his friends, his neighbors, his community and—most important of all—to the cause of Christ at home and abroad.

The Bible says: "Therefore, my brothers, I implore you by God's mercy to offer your very selves to him: a living sacrifice, dedicated and fit for his acceptance, the worship offered by mind and heart" (Romans 12:1, NEB). When a Christian dedicates himself to the Lord's service, certainly his pocketbook is included in the deal, as a part of the "living sacrifice."

Those with dedicated pocketbooks are the joyful Christians. We are told that God loves a cheerful giver. It is likewise true that he who loves God is sure to be a giver—a cheerful giver, a joyful giver. This means that the Christian will try to be frugal and discriminating in his expenditures on himself, in order to be generous in what he does for others.

Stingy with oneself, liberal with others, and bountiful in one's support of the Lord's work—that is the goal I recommend for myself and for others who serve Christ.

CHAPTER
7

CAVEAT VENDOR

RALPH WALDO EMERSON HAS GIVEN
the world many wise pronouncements. But the famous dictum attributed to him about the man with
the better mousetrap, when considered in a modern
context, somehow seems to be below the Emersonian
standard.

Mr. Emerson claimed that though the man with
a better mousetrap should build his house in the
woods, the world would make a beaten path to his
door. For one thing, it seems to me that "the world"
covers too much territory; it implies everybody—
athletes and tottering octogenarians; dukes, dowa-
gers, cowpunchers, United States senators, ophthal-
mologists, insurance salesmen, beggars, coloratura
sopranos—everyone.

If you can imagine all these people pouring into
the woods, trampling the wild flowers and forest sap-
lings as they go, grimly intent upon one thing—to
buy a mousetrap—you'll have, to say the least, quite
a picture. As a matter of fact, if in these days you
really want to buy a mousetrap, all you need to do is
to pick up one at the hardware store on the way
home from work; or dial that strange emporium, the
neighborhood drugstore, and let them deliver one,
along with the tooth paste, aspirin tablets, a baseball
for Junior, and a copy of *The Saturday Evening Post*.

Another thing—how do we know that the man in
the woods makes mousetraps at all, if he doesn't ad-

vertise his product? And even if we should accident-
ally hear about What's-his-name's mousetrap, why
should we feel an urge to buy it instead of some
standard, well-advertised brand?

There are listed in Thomas's *Register* numerous
manufacturers of mousetraps. It is doubtful that any
of them, whether they began their business in the
woods or elsewhere, would have survived till now had
they sat back and waited for an impatient mob to
beat a path to their doors.

There is no getting around the simple fact that if
you have a product to sell, you had better let folks
know about it. Also, if your product has any unique
advantages, you had better not be coy about saying
so; otherwise, you will lose a lot of business to competitors who are not shy about singing the praises of
their products. And remember that your competitors
can include merchants in any part of the world whose
products or services, although quite dissimilar to
yours, may nevertheless be competing for your prospects' dollars.

It is no wonder that advertising—this art of creating in the minds of people an impelling urge to buy
a particular product or service in preference to any
other product or service, similar or dissimilar—plays
so dominant a role in most businesses.

Advertising costs account for a large chunk of the
average company's annual expense budget; some corporations spend as much as $10,000,000 per year on
advertising. It is not unusual for an advertising budget to run as high as 10 per cent of a company's an-
ticipated sales for the year, and in two or three in-
stances the advertising-to-sales ratio has run as high
as 25 per cent. A few companies report that they

spend twice as much for advertising their products as for labor to produce them.

According to the *Economic Almanac,* magazine advertising in the United States for 1960 totaled $938,000,000 and newspaper advertising totaled $3,650,000,000. The sum of all expenditures for advertising in 1960 was about $11,600,000,000.[1]

These statistics have been cited to emphasize one point: In our free enterprise system, except for those companies that temporarily enjoy a patent monopoly, or that operate under a franchise or subsidy granted by some government, or that collude with competitor-friends to fix prices and to rig bids, competition is relentless and severe.

This never-ending competition finds expression in every department of a company's business—from engineering design through purchasing, production, and quality control, to sales and service. But the special emphasis these days is on sales. "More sales for more profits" seems to be the unwritten slogan of most concerns, the driving force behind most businessmen.

At this very moment, thousands of company executives are staring at sales charts and graphs, gloating if favorable results are indicated, and fretting if unfavorable. In the next twenty-four hours there will take place in this country thousands of sales conferences, luncheons, banquets, seminars, panel discussions. Hundreds of conventions, with much emphasis on selling something or other, will get under way early next week. About Thursday or Friday these conventions will come to an end, and the

[1] The *1962 Economic Almanac* (page 336) published by National Industrial Conference Board.

participants will wend their weary way homeward, leaving behind them the usual empty bottles, dirty ash trays, and wastebaskets full of discarded memoranda garnished with doodles.

Thousands of speeches will be delivered this month on the subject of sales. Thousands of articles of the same tenor will soon appear in periodicals. Hundreds of books concerned with salesmanship, advertising, and so forth, now in the process of being written, will soon take their places on the shelves beside hundreds of other books already written on the same subject.

There will be a thousand contests to choose the Salesman of the Year, and a thousand Salesmen of the Year, duly chosen, will be awarded the usual plaques; the usual pictures will be taken by bored newspaper photographers, and each picture will disclose a smiling MC looking vaguely at the smiling S.O.Y., who in turn will be looking vaguely at the plaque they hold between them.

And we must not forget to mention Miss Idaho Potato and Miss Butane, and the thousands of other handsome young ladies, soon to be crowned queens of their respective courts. Photographers will be busy taking *their* pictures, too, to be run in the same Sunday newspapers, but more prominently than the Salesman of the Year, because they are much prettier. All of this, of course, is for the purpose of selling more potatoes and more butane gas, and more of the thousand other products represented by the thousand other queens.

Millions of advertisements, running the gamut in subject matter from lipsticks to airplanes, and in style from sheer inspiration to the most abject blah, will cover page after page of our newspapers and magazines, infringe upon the time of impatient radio and TV fans, and shout at motorists from billboards strategically placed along city streets and amid scenes of rural beauty.

The emphasis now, more than ever before, is on Sales, Sales, Sales!

Why does this concern the Christian and his Christian principles? Because sales are made to people. You do not sell to a *thing*, but to a *person*, or a group of persons—to people.

The purchaser may be somebody you have never seen, never will see. Nevertheless, it is well to remember that he is a real person, who, because of his faith in you and in your claims, has decided to surrender a part of his working life to possess one of your products. If he is an average American worker, and if your price is $250, he is, in effect, giving up about two weeks of his working life to make the purchase. If it is a $18,000 house you are selling him, then your asking price is three years of his working life.

Whether you are selling ocean-going yachts to wealthy, fastidious sportsmen, or razor blades by the millions to millions of anonymous customers whose desire is to rid themselves of whiskers as quickly, comfortably and economically as possible—no matter what your "line" is—you are dealing with people. And every transaction that involves people involves moral considerations; therefore, anyone who has anything at all to sell will of necessity be faced with moral issues, must make moral decisions.

These decisions, I believe, may be put into one or the other of two broad classes: first, *what* a Christian should or should not sell; and, second, *how* a Christian must sell.

1. *What* a Christian can or cannot sell.

Certainly there are some kinds of merchandise with which a Christian can have no dealings whatever. For example, any man halfway worthy of the name of Christian would rather die of slow starvation than make a guaranteed fortune by peddling dope to teenagers, or selling pornographic literature or producing and exhibiting motion picture filth and violence of the "adult only" type.

For that matter, I know personally many men who, I truly believe, would rather face a firing squad than have any part in the sale of intoxicants, especially to juveniles.

These stalwart Christians, whatever you may think of their militant, unbending stand in such matters, are motivated by a sincere desire to please their Lord. They believe God's word, and try to live by it. They take seriously, for example, the Saviour's warning, as recorded in the Gospel according to Matthew: "Whoever receives one such child in my name receives me. But if a man is a cause of stumbling to one of these little ones who have faith in me, it would be better for him to have a millstone hung round his neck and be drowned in the depths of the sea. Alas for the world that such causes of stumbling arise! Come they must, but woe betide the man through whom they come!" (Matthew 18:5-7, NEB.)

Of course, it is easy for us to pick out a despicable and criminal activity, remote from our own experience, like selling marijuana to school children, to condemn and contemn. We who can have no conceivable temptation in such a direction and who would probably be too timid to risk the penalties of the law anyway, hardly deserve praise for not being dope peddlers. But what about a man engaged in a normal, legitimate business? Is he ever faced with moral decisions in this area of what to sell and what not to sell? Indeed he is—every businessman is.

Consider, for example, a Christian newspaper publisher. Quite often, I should imagine, he must decide against his own pocketbook and refuse space for unwholesome advertisements. Should he, in these modern times, persist in such a puritanical policy, or should he open his advertising columns to anyone who will pay for the space, then wink at the use to which the space is put?

In his news columns, shall he sell the public what the public wants? Shall he, in order to sell more newspapers, cater to our lower natures by devoting excessive space, in fullsome detail, to that which is bizarre, morbid, gruesome, gossipy, prurient, sensational? Should he make no effort to elevate the public tastes and moral standards other than by the excellent things he says on his editorial page, which, I am afraid, many of us really do not read and very few of us ponder?

What about a manufacturer who allows a weakness to remain in his product solely to increase future repair sales? What if, at no extra cost to himself, he can so improve his product as materially to reduce the upkeep expense to his customers? Shall he make the improvement or shall he "leave well enough alone"?

Incidentally, I know a manufacturer who about forty years ago declared that if he could produce a cotton gin feeder-cleaner so durable that he would never be able to sell a single replacement part for it, he would enthusiastically build such a machine. Ten years later, I was interested to learn that although his machines had to contend with rocks and other hard extraneous matter in the cotton, he had so well succeeded in his purpose that the upkeep cost per machine was averaging less than five dollars a year. Some of these early machines, now twenty-five years old, are still operating satisfactorily.

What does the Bible have to say on this general subject? Many apt verses from Scripture could be cited, but let me quote again Colossians 3:23, paraphrased in my own language: "Whatever you do in business, do only that which will please God. If you know that it will please Him, then do it heartily, enthusiastically."

Does anyone think that he can please God by selling for a profit something that is deliberately less than the very best he can produce? Or something that intentionally involves a latent defect or a hidden shoddiness? Or something that might harm the user or consumer?

It is far better, I submit, to lose sales volume than to lose the Lord's approval of what we are trying to sell. For what does it profit a Christian to be a big success in the eyes of some people, if at the same time he is a complete failure in the eyes of his Master? If we are ever called upon to make a choice between so-called success *without* God's approval, and failure *with* it, let us hope that we will have the courage and the wisdom to choose to fail.

2. *How* a Christian must sell.

A friend of mine, a successful sales executive, concludes a paper on "The Moral Aspects of Advertising" with these words:

I agree wholeheartedly with Francis Bacon that every man is a debtor to his own profession. This is especially true of the advertising man, who frequently has at his disposal almost unlimited funds with which to sway and influence the desires and decisions of millions of people. And of course the *Christian* advertising man, over and above his obligation to his business and to the public, has a supreme obligation to the Lord.

So in planning an advertisement, let's ask ourselves the usual questions. Is it simple and understandable? Is it brief enough to hold attention? Will it stand the test of time so we won't have to be ashamed of it tomorrow? Is it clear enough to get through to the prospect quickly and forcibly? Does it appeal to the heart and the head? Is it authoritative and does it carry conviction?

And then, when all these questions have been answered satisfactorily, let's imagine that the Lord Himself is asking for our personal, face-to-face answer to the most important question of them all, Is it the truth?

Is it the truth? That, simply stated, is the ultimate standard by which a Christian needs to judge every proposed piece of advertising material. Is it truthful, both in what it says and in what it implies? The Lord Himself asks the question each time, and each time it is to Him that the Christian must give his answer.

Is it the truth? is the sum and substance of an excellent code of ethics adopted jointly by the American Association of Advertising Agencies and the Association of National Advertisers. This code condemns seven practices which are defined as "advertising of an untruthful, indecent or otherwise objectionable character."

1. False statements or misleading exaggerations.
2. Indirect misrepresentation of a product or ser-

vice, through distortion of details, or of their true perspective, either editorially or pictorially.

3. Statements or suggestions offensive to public decency.

4. Statements which tend to undermine an industry by attributing to its products, generally, faults and weaknesses true only of a few.

5. Price claims that are misleading.

6. Pseudo-scientific advertising, including claims insufficiently supported by accepted authority, or that distort the true meaning or practicable application of a statement made by professional or scientific authority.

7. Testimonials which do not reflect the real choice of a competent witness.

In passing, it may be noted that six of these seven condemnations are covered by the Ninth Commandment, "Thou shalt not bear false witness against thy neighbour."

Is it true? is the very first question asked by the Rotary Four Way Test, a code which coincides with the fundamental principles involved in Jeremiah 9:23-24 and Philippians 4:8. This code, much used by responsible businessmen in the United States and many foreign lands, was devised by H. J. Taylor, a past president of Rotary International, "as a direct answer to prayer."

1. Is it the TRUTH?

2. Is it FAIR to all concerned?

3. Will it build GOOD WILL and BETTER FRIENDSHIPS?

4. Will it be BENEFICIAL to all concerned?[1]

If every sales policy and every proposed advertise-

[1] © 1946 R. I.

ment were subjected to and governed by this Four Way Test, or by any other test based on the teachings of Christ, American business would undergo some startling changes. For one thing, much of the merchandise being offered for sale would disappear from the market, because such a test presents a choice between truth and silence, and either truth or silence would be fatal to any product that has no merit.

Caveat Vendor. Let the seller beware—especially if he is a Christian. Let him be wary of himself, mostly, lest in his ambition to attain high sales volume he stoop to low methods of selling, or to selling something that should not be sold at all.

Let him concentrate his attention mainly on the quality of the product which he plans to offer the public, making sure that it will be a good investment for his customer—in other words, *"beneficial to all concerned."* Then, when he is sure that he has such a product, let him say so forcefully, but with dignity, good taste and, above all else, faithfulness to the *truth.* Let him contend in the market place for his full share of the business, but let him make certain that his tactics are *"fair to all concerned."* If he will do all this, the good will of his customers will come automatically and he will build many solid and lasting *friendships* for his company.

And, in the process, he may even discover that Mr. Emerson, if not taken too literally, was not altogether wrong after all when he made that crack about the better mousetrap.

MATÉRIEL
and PERSONNEL

ALMOST ANYONE PAST HIS FORTIETH birthday knows the therapeutic and philosophical value of a good rocking chair. The very thought of a fireside rocker on a winter's night suggests peace, security, contentment, and hospitality.

But if you are in the chair business and are trying to sell a rocking chair to a certain prospect, you will need a better basis of appeal than the prospect's fondness for rockers in general. *Your* rocker in particular must appeal to him more than anybody else's; he must be attracted to it because of its appearance, the way it is put together, its comfortable feel, and its price. But even that is not enough. Wait until he has bought the chair, and has rocked in it for a month or so; then, if he is still delighted with his purchase, you have without a doubt made a *successful* sale.

A legal sale has ordinarily been consummated when the purchaser has paid, or agreed to pay, for the article—whatever it may be—and has taken possession. But a *successful* sale has been made only when, after a sufficient time for testing, the customer has brought in his final and favorable verdict.

The testing period varies in length with different commodities. For a piece of apple pie, ten seconds will do, but several months may be necessary in the case of an automobile. When the customer has had time to put his purchase to the test, what will the verdict be? After the last bite of pie has gone the way of its predecessors, will he smack his lips gratefully and lay down his fork with a sigh of contentment? If so, the sale has been eminently successful. And will the customer, after using his new car for a month or so, still be boasting to his neighbors that it was a mighty good buy? If so, it will be in order then, but not until then, to ring up the successful sale of one automobile.

With the reader's kind indulgence, I shall illustrate my point by quoting three letters borrowed from my company's files. The letters pertain to one of our products, an automotive air conditioner; the three units involved were supposed to be identical in construction and should all have produced identical results. But actually, what a difference!

The first letter is from a lady in Arizona.

> Dear Sir:
> On July 27, 1960, a ——— ——— Unit was installed in my 8-cylinder Plymouth car. Since installation of this conditioner, it has been on the average taken in every two weeks to a service station because the equipment would lose its fluid. I have had to be without my car one full day. . . .
> I have purchased a lemon. . . . Several friends have purchased ——— ———'s because I was very enthusiastic about it. But now, I certainly cannot recommend it to anyone.
> I would appreciate hearing from you as to what you are going to do about the air conditioner, since I have made all the adjustments possible within the limits of the guarantee.
> > Yours truly,
> > Mrs. R. W.

The second letter is from a man in California:

Gentlemen:

Since July, 1960, at which time our ——————
—————— was installed, we have had almost
instant automotive air conditioning at the flick
of a switch. . . .

We have made desert trips through areas like
the Mojave Desert, during daylight hours in
August with our Buick Convertible, a 21 ft.
Oasis Vacation House Trailer and a 15 ft. Yellow
Jacket Boat on a 17 ft. trailer as a three vehicle
unit and experienced air conditioning much to
our comfort and satisfaction.

My wife and I agree that the —————— ——————
Unit would be the one auxiliary item that we
would not be without in any automobile we
may own in the future.

Sincerely yours,
C. E. T.

The third letter, brief as Caesar's *Veni, vidi, vici*
comment, is similarly to the point:

Gentlemen:

The air conditioner is working O.K. Cool, Cat,
Cool!

Yours truly,
O. W., Jr.

The people who wrote all three of these letters are,
I am sure, reasonable people. Then, why should two
of them have been delighted with their investment
while the third was temporarily (when she wrote the
letter) disgruntled with hers?

There can be only one answer: the air conditioners
the two men bought were normal, efficient units,
whereas the unit which the lady purchased was, un-

fortunately, a poor one—a "lemon," as she so frankly describes it.

But why was hers a poor unit? Why, in a family of a thousand or so identical counterparts would this one air conditioner turn out to be a black sheep, and all the rest of them good performers?

There are several possible explanations. Perhaps an engineer slighted a detail in adapting the basic unit to that particular make and model of automobile. Or an order clerk may have been careless in writing up the specifications. Or the quality control people may have permitted a faulty purchased component to get by them. Or perhaps an assembler was negligent, or an inspector careless about some item on his check-list. Or a field mechanic may have failed to follow factory instructions in making the installation. But this much is sure: someone—some *person*—in our organization "goofed."

Incidentally, when an employee goofs, the company's chief executive should assume a part of the blame himself, for the reason that he hired the goofer. He is responsible, directly or indirectly, for the selection and training of the company's employees. Therefore, if an order clerk, for example, makes a careless or stupid blunder, at least some of the blame may properly be charged to the company's president, because he chose the order clerk. If the corporation is a large one, he chose the man who chose the order clerk; or, if a very large corporation, he chose the man who chose the man who chose the man who chose the order clerk.

Behind every failure of *matériel* is always a failure of *personnel*.

And behind every success of matériel, there is invariably a vast amount of intense, painstaking, unrelenting effort by people, working as individuals and together as a coördinated team.

Consider, for example, the history of almost any kind of mechanical device—say, a new and needed household appliance. First, it begins as a dream in the mind of one man. This man discloses his dream to the management, and certain engineers are assigned to the new project. The dream now begins to take form on paper; tentative pencil sketches appear, followed soon by blueprints. The research and development people then build prototypes, one after another, and make tests with them, intent upon finding the very best possible embodiment of the idea— and there is only one best! Blueprints are revised, discarded and replaced by new prints, which in turn are revised, discarded and replaced. Meanwhile, many other folks of varied talents and training appear on the scene: design engineers, concerned with the "cosmetics" or aesthetic appearance of the device; production engineers, concerned with its adaptability to smooth and economical production in the preparatory departments and on the final assembly line; safety engineers, trying to avoid law suits for damages or injuries; specialists in painting, plating and packaging; purchasing people, shipping people, sales people, advertising consultants, patent lawyers, and scores of other experts, each making his own contribution to the collective concept.

And when this collective concept has been expressed in a final prototype, and the final prototype has satisfactorily met its performance trials, its accelerated torture tests, and all other tests, management gives the signal and a whole new series of activities is launched. Tool and die experts get busy making the tools, templates, gauges and other special equipment needed for large-scale production; the purchasing people begin to buy raw material and finished components for necessary working inventories; superintendents, foremen, assemblers, quality control specialists, packagers, shippers, invoice clerks, book-keeping-machine operators and many other people— perhaps hundreds or even thousands of them, in scores of categories— are soon concentrating their respective skills on their respective assignments.

Thus, from first to last, from its conception in one man's mind to its final expression as a bright, shining new appliance in the hands of salesmen throughout the country, the device has received the close attention of a great many people. It will have reached the marketplace at the cost of much sweat, many gray hairs, and many sleepless nights. The reward? If everyone has done his work well, the result will be public approval for the device. This means sales, and sales mean profits, and profits mean salaries, wages, dividends, bonuses and all the other material benefits that accrue under the American competitive system to those business teams that are intelligent, alert, industrious and persistent.

The manager's part in all this is similar to that of a coach on a football field. The manager, with the help of his carefully chosen staff, selects the members of the team, trains them in their respective and specific positions on the team, inspires them to play the game hard and enthusiastically against all competitors, devises the strategy and the tactics, and leads the team to what it is hoped will be a brilliant succession of victories.

The analogy can be carried further. We all know what happens to a coach who loses too many games. The same fate awaits a business manager who loses too many of *his* games.

If the manager and his assistants are Christians, they will do well to emulate some of those football teams that go into a close huddle before the game to invoke God's help. The first time I ever saw this was many years ago, just before Bo McMillan and the praying Colonels from Kentucky went out on the field against a much stronger team. I don't know what the boys prayed about, and at this late date I cannot remember whether they won or lost. But I do remember that they played a whale of a game.

And certainly I know what the Christian manager needs to pray for. He needs to pray for wisdom, courage, and an understanding heart. He needs to remember that he is directing a team whose members are not mere units or cogs, but real people, with real problems, who have placed in his hands themselves, their futures, and the welfare of their families. Unless he is a pompous and self-sufficient fellow, he will, in view of these responsibilities, feel strongly the need of divine help and guidance.

Yesterday I was present at the monthly meeting of our Employees' Advisory Committee. This committee has fifteen members, chosen by the vote of all factory employees, who hold office for one year. The chairman, Don McGrew, who works in our Inventory Department, called the meeting to order by asking everyone to stand for prayer to be led by Charlie Minter. In his prayer, Charlie, who is in the Pipe and Rod Department, thanked the Lord for the privilege of working together; interceded for some of our sick people, mentioning them by name; thanked the Lord for our company; and asked for *wisdom* not only for the members of the committee but also for the company's management. Then we all sat down and began to discuss some of our mutual problems, including the possibility of a general wage increase.

It was no rubber-stamp affair. There were differences of opinion but all matters that reached a final decision were decided unanimously. On one point I changed my view by reason of the arguments and supporting facts presented by two or three of the committee members.

As the fifteen people left the room together, we all felt that the meeting had been decidedly worthwhile and that the Lord had been present with us. If wisdom has anything to do with folks getting along with each other, then certainly Charlie Minter's prayer for wisdom had been answered.

Why shouldn't such a prayer be answered? Did not the Saviour Himself say, "Ask, and it shall be given you; seek, and ye shall find; knock, and it shall be opened unto you"? (Matthew 7:7.)

And does not the Bible also tell us that: "If any of you lack wisdom, let him ask of God, that giveth to all men liberally, and upbraideth not; and it shall be given him. But let him ask in faith, nothing wavering . . ."? (James 1:5-6.)

CHAPTER
9

THE SECRET—
GOOD PERSONNEL

THE SECRET OF GOOD PERSONNEL *relations* is good personnel.

The secret of good personnel *attitudes* is good personnel.

The secret of good personnel *performance* is good personnel.

The principal asset of any worthy business enterprise is good personnel.

These truisms are obvious—so much so that merely to mention them seems somewhat pontifical. And yet, if so obvious and true, why does the average businessman neglect them when he hires people to be lifetime members of his business team? Why don't we managers spend more time and effort in appraising the character of our prospective employees?

It may be that we are too lazy.

Or it may be that we have a false concept of human values. We may believe—wrongly, of course—that the most important asset a job applicant can bring with him is know-how, the result of natural ability plus previous training at someone else's expense. If we are too eager to acquire the applicant's know-how, we can easily persuade ourselves that certain flaws in his character are "minor in nature and effect and should be overlooked, at least in this instance."

Or it could be that some of us, feeling frustrated, have become cynical about old-fashioned virtues in modern human beings. Since we all fall far short of saintliness, why all this to-do about the character of one man in preference to another's? "Let's not bother with fine discriminations but give the job to the man with the most know-how."

Whatever the reason, it is readily apparent that in this modern technical age many employers are placing more importance on a man's experience and on his proficiency for the job at hand than upon his attitudes and character. I submit that this is wrong and, in the long run, unwise. I feel that what we need even more than clever *aptitude* tests for prospective employees, is reliable *rectitude* tests. We need to ask not only, "*Can* this man do this job?" but also, "Does he *want* to do this job?"; "Does he have a strong desire to do his work honestly and effectively?" Even more important than his aptitudes are his attitudes.

A man with the right attitudes and a reasonable amount of intelligence, plus a little help from management, will quickly acquire the necessary know-how for any ordinary job. But a man who lacks the right attitudes—in other words, a man of weak character—no matter how great his proficiency, or how high his IQ, or how superb his education, will prove to be worse than worthless. Such a man is the proverbial sow's ear, and cannot be made into a silk purse unless God does it by a miracle.

As for my team, I ask for no full-blown geniuses. Instead, give me simple, modest, God-fearing people, bred and reared by Christian parents, and having, preferably, sturdy grandparents as well. Such folks are the "good personnel" referred to in the beginning of this chapter. With a team composed of such people, even under mediocre leadership, I will guarantee good personnel relations, good personnel attitudes and good personnel performance. Such a team will play a good, hard, clean game and have a lot of fun in the process.

Of course, as time goes on, some of the ambitious youngsters will outgrow our team. When they have gone as far as they can go with our company, they may decide to leave us to take bigger jobs with bigger companies. Or they may go into business for themselves. In either case they will leave with our blessing and such help as we can give them. Their departure will make room for other youngsters equally worthy and no doubt equally ambitious.

Now, in what we have had to say about training versus character, it has been by no means our intention to decry the value of a formal education. Everybody will admit that a janitor and the company president should know how to read and write; a stenographer should know how to spell; a private secretary, as well as her boss, should have an extensive vocabulary; a mechanic, a bookkeeper, the traffic manager, and for that matter, everybody in the organization should have a working knowledge of arithmetic; a mechanical engineer should know his higher mathematics and his basic physics; an advertising man and every company officer who has much writing or speaking to do should have a pretty good understanding of English rhetoric and some knowledge of etymology.

But for those folks who have been unable to obtain college degrees, or even to go through high school, I offer as consoling and inspiring exhibits such men as

Henry Ford, Thomas Edison, Abraham Lincoln and the Apostle Peter. *They* managed to get themselves pretty well educated without the benefit of much formal schooling, and so can anyone else who is intelligent and sufficiently ambitious.

It has been my good fortune to know several useful and interesting people who, by choice or by force of circumstance, acquired their education the hard way. For example, there is Paul G., a former employee of our company, who during the sixteen years he worked for us dreamed of being a lawyer. While holding down his job as manager of our Repair Parts Department, he devoted his spare time to the study of law. His wife Betty, who shared her husband's ambition with him, worked in our Bookkeeping Department and thus helped with Paul's night school expenses. When the proud day arrived and Paul had received his license, he immediately left us to take a position in the City Attorney's office. After a term of service under an outstanding municipal lawyer, Paul has recently gone into private practice and, we are delighted to say, is doing well.

Then there is the case of an executive with whom I was closely associated for many years. This man's formal schooling had ended in the sixth grade of a country school in Tennessee. At fourteen years of age, he had taken a job in a brickyard, carrying and stacking bricks to help support the large family. Later he worked in a flour mill, then in a machine shop, and finally went into business for himself. Making full use of a short supply of leisure, he contrived by much reading and study to obtain a remarkably useful education, with the emphasis on economics, history and English literature. He acquired a splendid vocabulary by the simple process of reading completely through the dictionary, marking and studying those words which he felt could be useful to him. He became an outstanding inventor, manufacturer, banker, builder and church leader.

He was one of the most forceful and interesting talkers I have ever known. On one occasion it was my privilege to visit in his home when he was entertaining a famous editorial writer for one of our great national weeklies. As I sat before the fireplace and listened, spellbound, to the conversation of the two men on a wide range of subjects, I decided that it would be difficult indeed to determine which had the better education—the famous writer with his college degrees, or the man whose formal schooling had ended with the sixth grade.

Now, to point up my contention that it is unwise in recruiting or training personnel to subordinate character to schooling or education, let's imagine the same man at the personnel office of the great XYZ Corporation. He is, say, twenty-five years old. He presents himself before the interviewer and refers to the corporation's newspaper advertisement: "Mechanical Engineers Wanted." The interviewer is impressed with the young man; he likes his earnestness, his quiet enthusiasm, his obvious honesty. As the interview proceeds, it develops that our young friend has been attending night school for three years; that he has been doing some research work of his own in his "spare" time and has built a new type of dust collector. He has taken out two United States patents; he produces copies—would the gentleman like to see them?

No, the gentleman wouldn't. He has already spent

too much time with this one applicant. Many other applicants are waiting. So, pointing out that the management's specifications for the position require a degree in mechanical engineering from a reputable engineering college as well as five years of prior experience, he courteously dismisses our hero. And thereby, he dismisses several million dollars of profits for his company, and very likely its future president.

Why do I say its future president? Because I happen to know that this very man, when he was about forty-five or fifty years of age, was offered a top executive position with two famous corporations, one in Canada and the other in the United States. One of these positions, he was told, would lead shortly to the presidency of the company.

It is a good thing, of course, that the young man in our story did not get the job. He would never have been happy to be a mere social security number on the seniority list of Section 17, Department C, of the great XYZ Corporation. He would, for that matter, have liked neither social security nor the philosophy on which it is based. He would not have cared for the petty politics in Section 17, or for labor union rules and domination by labor union leaders. Like many other businessmen of his generation, he was an individualist. As such, he refused to be buried in the limbo of mediocrity.

He was the kind of man who usually votes Democratic when the Republicans are in power and Republican when the Democrats are in power. He feared God and had a deep respect for the United States Supreme Court—the old one, that is. He hated stupidity, snobbery and selfishness. He was a friend of the underprivileged and no respecter of persons.

In short, Dad was a "man of character."

When we speak of personal character, what do we have in mind? What type of character traits would you look for in an applicant if you were doing the hiring? I suggest to the reader that he make up a list of four or five qualities that he would particularly value in an employee. Here is my list:

1. Honesty
2. Gratitude
3. Enthusiasm
4. A competitive spirit

In the next four chapters, we shall try to make plain why we have chosen these particular traits of character above all others.

CHAPTER
10

"WHATSOEVER THINGS ARE HONEST"

A FEW YEARS AGO WE HAD A SMALL force of college students working at various night jobs in our factory. We felt that no supervision was necessary because all of the men were trusted and highly regarded. One of these was M. J. About a year after M. J. had left us and moved to another state, we received this surprising letter from him.

Dear Mr. Mitchell:
This is without doubt one of the most difficult letters I have ever had to write. The writing of it is not nearly so hard as was the coming to the place of willingness to write it.
The past few weeks and months have been the most thrilling in my Christian experience. At times I have felt as though the Lord were physically encircling me with His arms. . . . But along with this richness of fellowship has come the searchlight of the Word. This light has been brought to bear on several occasions when, as a nighttime employee of the John E. Mitchell Company, I came to work, punched in at the time clock, then left to do other things of my own choosing, and returned hours later to punch out and go home. This was just plain stealing. It was not only a sin against the Lord, but also

against the company. The Lord has already
graciously forgiven me, and at this time I ask
your forgiveness.

I have no idea the number of hours for which
you paid me that I did not work, but my guess
is that it would amount to a total of about $60.
At the present time, I am unable to pay you
this amount back, but as soon as I am financially
able I will send you the money.

Please pray for me that His will shall be carried
out completely in my life day by day.

Sincerely yours,
M. J.

To this we immediately replied:

Dear M:
Your letter of March 6th is a good letter, full of
Christian manliness and courage.

I assure you that the management of the Company forgives you for the wrong you have done.
But you are of course right in saying that it is
important for you to make restitution. Repent-
ance without restitution would be mere hypoc-
risy. I suggest that you send us a check for what
you think you owe us, whenever it is convenient
for you to do so.

We shall pray that the Lord will give you many
opportunities to serve Him and that you will
render a good account of yourself.

Sincerely yours,
J. E. M.

About six months later M. J. sent us his check for
$60, which we endorsed to his church and mailed
back to him.

All managers, even the dishonest ones, want their employees to be honest. In fact, they would probably place honesty at the head of their check-list for prospects.

The honesty we are talking about here is the old-fashioned kind. For fashions change in morals as in women's hats and hair-dos. For instance, it seems to be the current fashion among some sophisticates to sneer at the "quaint" religious ideas of our fathers. These devotees of Progress look down with a wan, tolerant smile upon anything connected with the faith of our fathers, and use such terms of derision as "old-fashioned individualism," "old-fashioned courtesy" and "old-fashioned honesty."

Now, what these critics mean by "old-fashioned honesty" is exactly what I mean, too—namely a scrupulous, punctilious, fine-haired, strait-laced sort of honesty. I mean the kind of honesty which, like God Himself, is "the same yesterday, today and forever."

Some cynic has said that every man has a price at which he can be bought. I don't believe it. I know many Christians who would scorn all the wealth in the world if offered in exchange for their immortal souls.

Besides, with most of us it is not the big money that tests our honesty so much as the nickels, dimes and quarters. For example, a man who would never be tempted to embezzle $10,000 from his employer might have no scruples about swiping towels from the hotel, or accepting too much change from the cashier, or permitting a mistake to be made in his favor on his paycheck, or writing on his expense account $1.05

for breakfast instead of the 70 cents which it actually costs him.

What does such a man say to his conscience? Probably something like this: "This hotel is bad about overcharging. I'll get a small part of it back by taking a towel or two as souvenirs." Or, "That lunch was not very good. I'll just keep this extra quarter as a sort of refund." Or, "Look at the way the government wastes our money! Besides, they'll never miss the tax on this little $12 cash item. Anyway, I'll bet everybody else is doing this sort of thing." Or, "This company doesn't pay me what I am worth; so why shouldn't I collect a small part of what is due me by upping some of my expense items?"

It is in the area of intangibles that the average man is most prone to dishonesty. What, for example, about our misuse of that valuable commodity we call time? An employee who steals time is as much a thief as one who steals a can of paint or an S-wrench. By appropriating for his own use or by frittering away five minutes of paid-for time each day, an employee in reality is stealing from his company more than $50 a year. That is enough, if it were cash instead of time, to make a man, in some states, indictable for grand larceny.

We once had an employee named Gardner. One day it was brought to our attention that Gardner frequently stayed at his bench five or ten minutes past the quitting bell, for which he received no pay. Out of curiosity we investigated and found that this was simply Mr. Gardner's way of making sure that he put in all the time he was being paid for. He was that kind of Christian whose main purpose in what he did and said was to please the Lord. He wanted to be sure not to shortchange God. And so he was honest with an old-fashioned, second-mile sort of honesty.

Are we perfectly honest about our oral commitments? Do we make promises and engagements with our mental fingers crossed? Do we say, "I'll be there," feeling all the time that we will not be?

How honest are we in the matter of assuming unearned credit? Do we remain silent when someone commends us for an accomplishment or credits us with a good suggestion when we know all the time that the commendation or credit belongs elsewhere? Do we remain silent when someone else is blamed for a mistake that should rightfully be charged to us?

Every employer wants every employee to be honest. But what about the employer's own standards of integrity? Have not the workers the right to expect their boss to be a man of honor himself? A company, unless it is honest with its employees, customers, suppliers and the government, has no right to demand honesty of its employees, or of anybody else.

As a final illustration of what we mean by "old-fashioned" or second-mile honesty, let me recount a story that I heard a few years ago when active in Boy Scout work. The story is about a youngster named Jose who came from a large and very poor Mexican family living in a Dallas slum. The Scout Master who worked in that area became interested in Jose, got Jose interested in Scouting, outfitted him with a uniform, and started him on his way to earning a series of merit badges. One day as he was going home from school, Jose saw a wallet lying in the gutter. He picked it up and opened it, and looked at the contents. He had found a considerable sum of money. We don't know just what went through Jose's mind when he saw all that money, but we do know what he did with it. He turned it in at the police station.

Later someone asked his mother why he did it. Her reply was: "Jose is a Boy Scout. He thought that's what a Boy Scout was supposed to do. And, by the way, ain't that what *any of us* are supposed to do, if we find money that don't belong to us?"

Well, ain't it?

CHAPTER
11

WHERE ARE the NINE?

TEN LEPERS, OUTCAST AND FORLORN, were huddled outside a village when Jesus passed that way. "Jesus, Master, have mercy on us!"; "Help us, Lord!" they cried. The Lord, moved with compassion, instructed them to show themselves to the priest as evidence that they had been healed. They obeyed and as they went on their way, they *were* healed. One of them, full of gratitude, hurried back to Jesus and falling at Jesus' feet worshiped Him. Jesus' comment was, in effect: "Were there not ten lepers cleansed? Only this man has returned to give glory to God. Where are the nine?"

The same question might be asked today: "Where are the nine?"

The longer I live, the more convinced I become that gratitude is a rare and noble virtue, worthy to be admired in others and cultivated in ourselves. On the other hand, ingratitude is one of the most destructive and despicable of vices.

Gratitude produces fine sons and daughters, fine parents, fine husbands and wives, fine neighbors, fine citizens.

My home town, Dallas, has for many years been blessed with honest, unselfish, efficient government. One of the best mayors we have ever had is Robert L. Thornton, who recently completed his fourth term. I have heard Mr. Thornton say on many occasions:

"I cannot possibly do enough for Dallas, because Dallas has done so much for me." A grateful man, a great servant, a great mayor.

Gratitude produces patriots like Nathan Hale, whose only regret was that he had but one life to lose for his country. It is the distinguishing mark of Christian martyrs and missionary heroes. In fact, the force that impels all true Christian service is the Christian's gratitude for what his Saviour and Lord has done for him.

A good employee is grateful, whether he knows how to say so or not. He is grateful for the freedom to work or not to work. He is grateful to God for good health which permits him to work. He is grateful for his job—if not, he should lose no time in looking for another.

To illustrate what we have been talking about, here are three letters—chosen from many in our files —written by employees, or ex-employees or relatives of employees.

First, a letter from a sixteen-year-old boy who worked last year at a summertime job:

> Dear Mr. Roden:
> Thank you so very much for the many things that you have done for me this summer while I have been working for John E. Mitchell Company. I have enjoyed working and sincerely appreciate the opportunities I have had. I surely hope that I will be able to work again next summer—under you.
>
> Sincerely,
> Donald C. Grant

One from a daughter of a seventy-five-year-old employee:

Dear Mr. Mitchell:
I want to express my thanks to you for the most enjoyable afternoon and evening I spent with Mother and Daddy (R. C. Johnson) at the Mitchell employee's annual picnic last month. My father has spoken highly of you and . . . once again I thank you for letting him work on past the regular retirement age. It is his life. He loves to work and would be lost without it.
                              Sincerely,
                              Mrs. J. C. Wright

This one is from an assembly line foreman:

Dear Sir:
I have enjoyed working for the company for the past seventeen years. May God richly bless and keep you all and may you have many more years of success and happiness.
                              Yours truly,
                              Pat Slagle

This matter of gratitude should be mutual between management and employees. I meant every word of what I said in a letter addressed to our employees a few years ago, which reads as follows:

This morning while I was waiting for my cook, who is also my wife, to stir up a little breakfast, I wrote down a few paragraphs about a man whom I admire and like very much. He works for the John E. Mitchell Company. Let's see if you can guess who he is.

He has been with the company for several years, and during that time has worked in many different departments. Although no doubt he likes some kinds of work better than other kinds, he has never complained, but has given each job the closest attention and the best effort he can summon.

He is honest. His fellow workers need have no fear about leaving their lockers open around him. He is honest with the company, too. Realizing that time is money, he is careful to put in each day not 7 hours and 48 minutes, but 8 full hours.

He is intelligent. And being intelligent, he knows that whatever helps the company helps him. So he studies his particular job, and figures out ways to do it better, and more safely.

He is proud. He thinks he can turn out more work than the next man, and tries to prove it. He knows he can turn out good work. Therefore, he takes pride in his product. He is careful about his own appearance and the appearance of his work space—his part of the plant. He is proud of his department.

My friend is considerate. He takes great pleasure in helping the new fellow. You'd think the new fellow was some close relative of his, the way he shows him some of the tricks of the business. In fact, he helps everybody around him, apparently getting a big kick out of other people's success and happiness. This spirit is, of course, in evidence on occasions like United Fund Day; he gives his time with enthusiasm, as though helping some unknown people in need is not a chore, but a real privilege and joy.

He is loyal. The Mitchell Company, and the

fellows who work here, have faults—lots of 'em —but if an outsider talked to our friend in the Mitchell Company he'd never find it out. No sir, according to him it's the greatest outfit in Texas, and the fellows who work here are the grandest group of men you'll find anywhere. Reckon he figures that if a fellow can't be loyal toward his company, through thick and thin and ups and downs, he ought to go somewhere else where he can be loyal and work with folks he does like.

Our friend is enthusiastic. He has an inward glow and warmth that make you wonder a little. You wonder if he is turning in a job, day after day, for somebody much more important than the superintendent—somebody vastly more important than the president of the company. Is it possible that he is trying to please the Big Boss? Is it his ambition so to perform his task that he will hear, deep down in his heart, encouraging words from God Himself? Is it his desire above all else to hear the Saviour say to him: "Well done, thou good and faithful servant"?

Whatever goes on inside, whatever produces that warmth and glow, it is very apparent to us all that our friend is honest, intelligent, proud of his work, considerate of others, loyal to his company and enthusiastic. It is also apparent to us all that he is a valuable man, and one that we all like to have around.

Who is this man? The chances are, ten to one, that he is you. For the man I have described is no one in particular but is, I firmly believe, a typical member of the Mitchell working force. God bless him and all like him in America.

Gratitude, flowing in both directions between employers and employees, makes for mutual understanding and can easily lead to real affection and delightful fellowship.

Of course, there must be sound reasons for an employee to feel grateful to his company. It is up to management to provide these reasons. We will deal with this subject in a later chapter.

CHAPTER
12

FERVENT in SPIRIT

You will find enthusiasm on almost everybody's list of preferred character traits. "Nothing great was ever accomplished," says Emerson, "without enthusiasm."

But what is it? Particularly, what do we mean when we refer to the enthusiasm of workers in a factory or office? We suggest that enthusiasm is a compound of many ingredients: zeal, curiosity, imagination, desire to excel, pride of performance, excitement, fun.

Let us illustrate with two men, Joe and Bill. Both are operators of electric spot-welding machines. They have the same seniority, the same high-school education, practically the same aptitudes.

Joe rather likes his job. After all, it doesn't require too much physical or mental effort; in fact, he can now go through the motions automatically. This leaves him time for his own private reflections. He likes to think, as he works, about his little family, his home, the neighbors, church affairs, football, and so forth. Let's listen in on one of his reveries. "Boy!" he says to himself, "that was some game last night! Two touchdowns for Joe, Jr. Am I proud of that boy! . . . I sure wish I could buy that new car he wants us to get. But what about the down payment? . . . If only the company would give me another raise! . . . Wonder what old Bill's wage rate is. Look at him over there, working as hard as if he owned the company himself. Right now he is starting to weld another bracket that will take at least three minutes to finish, and there are only two minutes to quitting time . . . guess I'll start tapering off . . . there goes the bell! . . . So long, Bill, I'm shoving off. See you tomorrow."

Joe is a good man, but a little below our average worker. He has enthusiasm for some things, but not for his job! He lacks the spark.

But Bill *has* the spark. After three years he finds his job more fascinating and challenging than ever. . . . "It's funny how much there is to learn about this burning two pieces of metal together with an electric current," he says to himself. . . . "I wonder why we use castings and arc-weld them together, instead of using formed steel parts and spot welding them; think I'll have to find out. . . . Well, that was a pretty good record I hung up yesterday—240 cases in eight hours. Not bad, Bill, old boy, if I do say it myself. . . . And if I could get this jig changed so that the bracket would be on the left side instead of the right, I'll bet I could knock out 275 cases. Think I'll talk to the superintendent about this, when. . . . Say is that the bell already? So long, Joe. . . ."

A few minutes later Bill is on the way to the parking lot, carrying a library book on arc welding and a couple of technical magazines that he has borrowed from the superintendent. For some time Bill has been reading everything on the subject he can lay his hands on. Already, he knows more about spot welding technique than almost anybody in the company. That's his aim—to excel. He wants to be the best. Because of more pay? Yes, but not altogether that. Just for the fun of it. It's a game with Bill—a game that he wants to win. That's why Bill's day passes quickly. He finds the job fascinating and exciting. When he is promoted to foreman, which is inevitable, he will sail into his new responsibilities with the same fervency of spirit. In short, Bill is enthusiastic.

It is our privilege at the Mitchell Company to provide part-time work for about fifty students of the Dallas Theological Seminary. Most of these men work at the factory twenty-four hours or so each week during the school period and forty hours or more during the vacation period. They need the extra money to get themselves through school; besides, some of them have families to support.

All of these men are college graduates, and many were successful engineers, salesmen or business administrators when they responded to God's call to serve Him in a full-time ministry. I dare say that hardly anywhere else in the country will you find men polishing floors and emptying wastebaskets, who not only have at least four years of higher education but also are presently engaged in a four-year course of study in Hebrew, Greek, English Bible, Christian doctrine, homiletics, and so forth.

And I also dare say that nowhere in the country will you find office floors better cared for than here at the Mitchell Company. The reason is simple. These men know, believe and live by the Scriptures. For instance, they know all about Romans 12:11: "Not slothful in business; fervent in spirit; serving the Lord." So, out of gratitude to the Lord for providing them with their temporary, much-needed work, they serve Him with brooms, mops and other tools—fervently, enthusiastically.

An enthusiastic man learns faster, does his work better, and in the right kind of an organization progresses more rapidly than the mere hack worker to whom every job is another form of drudgery. Incidentally, the enthusiastic man is almost invariably a happy man.

CHAPTER
13

A COMPETITIVE
SPIRIT

THE AVERAGE AMERICAN LOVES COM-
petitive games and he loves to win. Suggest almost
any conceivable kind of a pastime and you will find
Americans engaged in it, somewhere.

Americans of various ages are ready to compete,
one against one, as in wrestling, handball, chess,
tick-tack-toe; or two against two, as in tennis; or five
against five, as in basketball; or nine against nine, as
in baseball; or eleven against eleven, as in football;
or one against many, as in the mile run, a pie-eating
contest, a spelling bee; or one against all comers, as
in a competition to determine who can swim the
Channel in the shortest time, or who can sit at the
top of a flagpole for the longest time, or who can get
to the moon first.

If necessary, a man will even compete against an
imaginary opponent as in solitaire against old Sol,
or in golf against Par or Colonel Bogey.

Name your "weapons," and issue a challenge, and
Americans somewhere will respond, eager to compete. For example, produce a set of horseshoes, and
someone will try to beat you tossing them at a stake;
a pole, and someone will try to jump higher with it
than you can; tiddlywinks, and someone will try to
flip the yellow ones into the cup before you can flip

in the green ones; a bag full of gas and someone will try to set an altitude record with it, riding in the basket attached. You will find competition in throwing stones or swinging an axe, in turtle racing, in frog jumping, in cock fighting, in hog calling, in calf roping, in corn husking, in snake killing, in jumping over barrels or in hitting anything that's round with a variety of sticks, bats, cues, clubs, mallets, rackets and paddles.

If a man is too lazy to engage in firsthand competition, there are many forms of vicarious competition available for him. He can jam himself with 50,000 other people into a baseball park and root for the "home team" whose players, by the way, all hail from distant cities. Or, if a man is lazier still, he can sit in front of his TV set and watch two young gentlemen intent upon the obliteration of each other's features in a boxing match.

When this spirit of competition so much in evidence in Americans at *play* takes hold of Americans at *work,* you can expect production records to be broken. I witnessed an example of this one day in 1918, in a hay-unloading contest. My outfit, the Second Battalion of the 138th Infantry, stationed at a camp near Ft. Sill, Oklahoma, was assigned the task of unloading several carloads of baled hay. We were told that the bales must be removed from the cars, carried a distance of about 100 yards and stacked neatly in high pyramids. Almost at the outset, a sergeant in Company H said something boastful to a corporal of Company G. Out of the ensuing banter there came a challenge, and soon all four companies were competing with each other to see which one could finish its assignment first. Various systems were

worked out on the spot. I do not remember which
system proved to be the best or which company won.
But I do know that never in the history of the world
has hay been unloaded and stacked any faster than it
was on that sweltering afternoon in Oklahoma by the
men of the Second Battalion, 138th Infantry Regi-
ment.

A competitive spirit in the employees of a business
enterprise not only increases output, but also makes
an exciting game of the activity, whatever it may be.
This is good, whether the competition is on a man-
to-man basis with emphasis on *personal* ambition, or
on a company-against-company basis with emphasis
on *team* ambition.

As a matter of fact, there is no conflict of interest
between the right kind of personal ambition and
the right kind of team ambition, anyway. Whatever
works for the good of a properly managed company
benefits all its employees. Certainly, no one employee
can be successful if his company is skidding toward
bankruptcy. Intelligent employees working with an
intelligent management know this, and therefore are
willing to subordinate personal ambition to the welfare of the team as a whole.

During World War II, our firm found it difficult
to obtain a defense contract. The folks in Washington
apparently looked askance at unknown manufacturers deep in the heart of Texas. But at last we got our
chance; we were awarded a small contract by the
Bureau of Naval Ordnance for the production of anti-
aircraft shells. We called all our people together and
made the announcement. We told them that it was
our ambition to prove to the Navy that Texas cow-
boys and Texas farm hands *could* produce excellent

war matériel; that we could certainly do as well as anybody else, if not better; that we particularly wanted to win for the Mitchell team the coveted Army-Navy E, an award for manufacturing excellence.

The challenge took hold and all the men and women jumped on the project with great enthusiasm. Many mistakes were made, of course, but somehow the spirit of the team overcame the errors of individuals.

Units within the organization began competing with other units. Our big 3½-inch 8-spindle automatic screw machines went into competition with each other. The crews adopted names for their machines such as "Hungry Harry," "The Sarge," "The Gob." A record board was hung above each machine and in each department, and on this board was printed in large figures the all-time production record of that particular group of workers. Somewhere we had acquired a bronze ship's bell and it was agreed that whenever a team broke its own record, the president of the company was to take this ship's bell to the department involved, climb a ladder and hang the bell from a hook fastened at the bottom of the record board. The bell was to remain with that particular crew until some other team broke *their* record. When that happened the president had to carry the bell to the work area of the new record holder and hang it on *their* hook. The team in possession rang the bell at coffee breaks, lunch and quitting time. And they rang it with gusto.

All this sounds a little silly and undignified. But it worked. For a while, records were broken so fast that the bell's tenure with any one record-holder had to be limited to one day. And even then, the bell was usually reserved and scheduled for several days, once for twelve days, in advance.

During the first month of operations under the Navy contract, we went heavily into the red. This made the management quite nervous. We began to wonder if we had estimated our costs too low. During the second month, however, the rate of production began to climb, and our costs came down. It was soon evident that we were not going to lose money on the job, after all. In fact, as our production continued to zoom, we became concerned in the other direction—about too much, rather than too little, profit. Finally we decided, although somewhat reluctantly, that our quoted price was too high. So, we voluntarily reduced the price, back to the date of the contract.

If all this sounds to the reader like boasting, I hasten to assure him that we intend it so. Why shouldn't a man be proud of being a fellow worker with the finest group of working men and women to be found anywhere?

And while we are boasting, let me add that due to this competitive spirit among units in the organization, and due to the competitive spirit in the company as a whole, we not only won the Army-Navy E once, but five times.

Furthermore, this spirit of teamwork carried us into many other fields of competition. We vowed that if we heard of any kind of a contest that was open to us as a competitor, we would enter that contest with the idea of winning it too. We decided that we wanted one of every kind of an award that was available. As a result, we led Dallas County in the number of pints of blood donated per capita to the Blood Bank; we had a record of 100 per cent participation in the Savings Bond campaign; we began a series of Community Chest Days, lasting from then until now, in which we averaged one day's pay for every person on the payroll; we twice won awards for safety (each time for one million man-hours without a lost-time accident); also citations for "Employ the Handicapped" programs; Red Cross flags; and many other awards. Our plant, although small and obscure, was visited by governors, mayors, admirals, generals, and once by the head of the National War Production Board. All of this was quite exciting and helped build up an *esprit de corps* similar to that enjoyed by the First Marine Division.

The competitive American spirit, properly directed and controlled, can accomplish remarkable results in work as well as in play. And it not only causes production rates to climb, but it also keeps the business from being humdrum and boring, adds zest and downright fun, promotes pride in the work, and a spirit of camaraderie among the workers, increases profits, wages and year-end bonuses.

Competition is good, and a competitive spirit, if tempered with common sense, is an extremely valuable asset for an employee to possess.

CHAPTER
14

WHAT MANNER
of MAN IS THIS?

GRANTED THAT A SPIRIT OF GRATITUDE, strait-laced honesty, enthusiasm, a competitive attitude and a capacity for teamwork are all important traits of character, how does one go about finding out whether and to what extent a prospective employee may possess them? What can one learn about a stranger's character in a thirty-minute contact?

Much. By merely asking some apparently casual questions and by listening carefully to the applicant's answers and prompting him to expand upon them, a skillful interviewer can learn a great deal, indeed.

Here are a few sample questions.

● Mr. Smith, if you had a city-wide choice, what kind of a company would you like to work for?

● What would you like our company to do for you besides giving you the job you are applying for?

● If *you* were an employer, Mr. Smith, what traits of character would you want an employee to have?

● Why do you think we should hire you in preference to other candidates for this job?

● Mr. Smith, what do you like to do in your leisure time?

As the interview proceeds, let's observe *how* Mr. Smith replies to our questions. Is he too glib? Is he obviously trying to make an impression upon us, in-

115

stead of stating the simple truth? Does he constantly
use such expressions as "To tell you the truth," "To
be perfectly frank about it," "I'll be honest with you,"
and the like? If so, we can be pretty sure that he is
not frank, or truthful, or honest. Real honesty does
not need self-advertising; it is the fruit of spiritual
influences quietly at work in a man's heart.

Mr. Smith's replies to any questions that we may
ask him regarding his leisure and his hobbies will
probably give us some interesting sidelights on his
character and his qualifications. What a man does
with his spare time *off* the job is a good index of how
he will spend his working time *on* the job.

Leisure has assumed an awesome significance in
today's America. We of this generation have at least
thirty hours more free time per week at our disposal
than our fathers, only fifty years ago, had at theirs.
This has been caused by the change from a sixty-hour
work week which prevailed then to the forty-hour
week which prevails now; by the mechanization of
those household chores which required so much of
their time and effort to do manually; and by the fact
that we need less sleep than they needed, because we
work less and are not so bone-tired by nightfall as they
were.

There is now some talk about legalizing and adopt-
ing a thirty-two-hour work week. When this has come
to pass, we will find ourselves spending, out of the
total hours available each week, 20 per cent at work,
40 per cent in sleeping and eating, and 40 per cent as
we please.

All of us have heard sermons urging us to "remember the sabbath day, to keep it holy." It is very
seldom, however, that the preacher emphasizes the
other part of the Fourth Commandment, which is:

"Six days shalt thou *labour,* and do all thy *work."*
Apparently, the average American nowadays prefers
his own version: "Four days shalt thou labour and do
thy work; the other three shall be holidays to spend
in any way that it may please thee."

There is nothing wrong with a little leisure, provided we contrive to spend it for our own physical
and mental and spiritual improvement, or for the
benefit of others, or for the glory of God. But if
the best we can do with it is merely to stare at third-
rate movies, or to worship at the TV shrine, or to read
trashy literature, or to sit in the semi-darkness of
some barroom, sipping Martinis and telling dirty
jokes, let's give it back to the Indians in exchange
for the work-time we have surrendered.

Certainly, a man cannot get into much trouble
while he is at work or asleep; it is by the misuse of
his leisure hours, and by the habits thus formed, that
he softens his character and runs the risk of making
a moral sissy of himself.

Especially is this true of our youngsters. We adults
are so preoccupied with our gadgets—these wonderful
things that need only plugging in, or switching on, or
cranking up, to go to work for our amusement and
pleasure—that we cannot find time to rear our children as they should be reared. To get them out of
our way, we turn some of the gadgets over to them.
Is it any wonder that we are beginning to harvest a
crop of irresponsible, indolent, selfish loafers and
spongers?

Of course, there are many exceptions to this gen-
erality. Thank God for these exceptions! Thank God
for the newspaper boys, especially those who arise at
five o'clock to throw the morning papers; for the kids
who work evenings and Saturdays in the neighbor-

hood grocery stores; for the yard boys; and for all
those other youngsters who have learned the value
of work. As long as our boys and girls are working
hard at school, at home, at church, or at some health-
ful form of exercise, we do not need to worry about
them. But when we adults abdicate our parental responsibilities and quit teaching the kids how to enjoy
work, we do a great injustice to them, to ourselves and
to our community. The real cause of juvenile delinquency is the delinquency of adults.

Let's have done with such Commencement Day
platitudes as, "The future of America rests with the
youth of today." Of course it does; anybody a few
years past diaper age would know that. Let's also forget such bromides as, "My generation has made a
failure of its responsibilities, but I hope that your
generation will do a better job." We are not dead
yet! *We are still the present generation.* Let's clean
up our own lives and devote some of *our* leisure
hours to the youngsters in such activities as Scouting,
Sunday school classes, Young Life Clubs and camps,
and so forth. Let's quit whining and get to work on
ourselves, and then on and with our youngsters.

The use that a man makes of his leisure not only
indicates what kind of a man he *is* but also, in a large
measure, determines what kind of a man he *will* be.
For both reasons, it is advisable in interviewing a
job-seeker to learn all that we can about how he em-
ploys his spare time.

Is there no way to get a line on a prospect for employment other than by interviewing him? What
about letters of reference?

Our experience with letters of reference is that they have no value whatever unless one knows the writer personally and is able to follow up by an interview with him. Even then, it is difficult to obtain a true picture of the candidate's character, because goodhearted people are prone to play up a man's strong points and to play down his weaknesses.

In the Mitchell Company we make use of what we call the sponsor system. It is a rule with us to hire only people recommended and endorsed by someone already working for the company. Under this old-fashioned system, we find that the sponsor is likely to be very careful about his recommendations. In the first place, he realizes how important it is, for the sake of his own pocketbook as well as in the company's interest, for us not to employ loafers, shirkers or sneaks. In the second place, he knows that he is putting his reputation and judgment on the line with the company officials. He knows that if he should wilfully or carelessly recommend some unworthy fellow for a job with us, we will pay no attention to his future recommendations—so he is careful whom he recommends.

As a matter of fact, in those rare cases when a new employee fails to live up to his sponsor's commendation, we not only work with the new man, but we also call in the sponsor and tell him wherein his protegé is failing. Very often the sponsor will say, "You leave this to me: I'll straighten him out." And very often he does just that!

CHAPTER
15

THE LINES of COMMUNICATION

EVERY EMPLOYEE WHO IS WORTH HIS salt likes to feel that he is a part of the organization he works for, and an important part too. He wants to be kept informed as to the company's progress, its prospects, and to some extent its problems. He likes to know about new items in the Research and Development Departments. He likes to have "advance information" concerning anything about the company that is new and interesting.

A wise management will do what it can to foster and encourage these attitudes in its employees. And management's success or failure in this area can be measured by the personal pronouns which are used by the average employee when he refers to the company. Is it *they* and *their,* or is it *our, us* and *my?*

There are of course many media available for communication between a company and its employees, such as house organs and other publications for employee circulation, bulletin boards, employees' meetings, employee committees, direct contact with foremen and labor union representatives, letters mailed to the homes of the employees, and others.

For large corporations, a house organ is an excellent means of communication. I have on my desk before me a copy of the LTV News, an excellent periodical published for the employees of Ling-Temco-Vought, Inc. It is a four-page paper, each page 11 inches by 17½ inches and chock-full of news regarding personnel, plans, progress of the company, and photographs. The place of honor in this particular issue, which is dated March 2, 1962, is a fine picture of the famous astronaut, Colonel John H. Glenn, taken about five years ago just after he had flown across the continent in a Chance Vought F8U-1 Crusader in the record-breaking time of 3 hours and 23 minutes.

There are many articles in the LTV News which, we judge, would be of great interest to the company's employees. They appear under such headlines as "Congratulations Go to Astronaut," "Penny Saved, Penny Earned for Company," "Employees Share Top Suggestion Award," "New LTV Credit Union All Ready for Business," "Altec Granted Patents for Telephone System," "Retirees Ready to Travel, Fish, Rest," "81 Pints Contributed to Vought Blood Bank," and "Swap Shop"—a section given over to items for sale or purchase.

Personal letters, especially if sent to the home, can be quite effective too. Never underestimate the importance of the wives and their good will. In the Mitchell Company, our married men have been blessed, for the most part, with unusually good wives; these ladies certainly deserve to be included in our greetings and good wishes. Why not, for example, a week or so before the annual picnic write a letter to Mr. *and* Mrs. Employee telling them that we expect the picnic this year to be the best ever and hope that they will be there, with the whole family? "We have again engaged the services of Mack, the barbecue man; there will be plenty of good barbecued beef and fried chicken and all the trimmings. The youngsters, as usual, will get a big bang out of the free rides on the Midway; the roller coaster, the merry-go-round, and all the others. So will you, if you are brave enough. If you are conservative, like me, you will prefer to sit around and watch the kids enjoy themselves. It will be good to see you all again."

About two years ago we adopted the practice of sending birthday greetings to employees a day or two before their birthdays. At the rate of one or two cards a day, the time required was, on the average, about five minutes per day. It is time well spent. For one thing, it gives the president of the company an opportunity to convey his interest in and esteem for the employee. In the second place, the average man likes to have some notice taken of his birthday. So, for that matter, does the average lady—provided too much fuss is not made about her actual age.

Once a year the employees of the Mitchell Company hold a company-wide election to determine who their committeemen shall be for the ensuing year. These committees, which play an important part in the life of the company, are briefly described in the paragraphs that follow.

The Employees' Advisory Committee is composed of the chairmen of all the other committees. Its own chairman is specifically selected by the employees at their annual election. Its members represent the employees' interests to management, and management's interests to the employees.

The committee meets once a month in the directors' room, the president of the company and two or three other executives being present. The chairman first calls for a report from each member on the work of his own committee. Grievances of a general nature are presented to the company's executives and often are handled then and there. For example, at a recent meeting it developed that one of the restrooms needed modernizing. The president agreed, and immediately assigned the undertaking to the Buildings Committee.

The company officials usually talk freely about programs, plans and policies, permitting the committee members to be the avenue of communication to the employees at large.

The Pension Committee, composed of four employees and three company officers, has charge of the Retirement Fund, is responsible for the payment of retirement benefits, and makes decisions in regard to special cases involving disability, and so forth.

The Safety and Good Housekeeping Committee investigates each injury to an employee, takes steps to avoid a recurrence, and is generally charged with the responsibility of making our plant a safe and pleasant place in which to work. The committee meets once a month; advisory members are the president of the company, the general superintendent, and two other executives.

The Sick and Welfare Committee administers the Sick and Welfare Fund, arranges for flowers to be sent to employees, or near relatives, in the hospital, and to funeral services in case of death; notifies the chaplain of all sick people so that he may add their names to his visitation list; and administers the Flower Fund, which is supported by the operation of vending machines in the plant.

The Sports and Entertainment Committee has

charge of all details of the company's annual picnic, all bowling tournaments and other athletic events.

The Bulletin Committee is responsible for the preparation and publication of the Mitchell Weekly Bulletin.

The Parking and Buildings Committee makes recommendations to management concerning parking facilities and enforces rules regarding the use of the five parking lots.

Incidentally, since we are located only two blocks from the State Fair grounds, parking space in our neighborhood is greatly in demand during special holiday events, such as a big football game in the Cotton Bowl. Under the auspices of the Parking and Buildings Committee, we throw open our parking facilities on these holiday occasions, free of charge. Visitors who take advantage of this service seem to be very appreciative, as attested by letters of thanks we have received from various sections of the country.

The United Fund Committee has charge of our United Fund Day at the Mitchell plant. This is a Saturday, usually late in March or early in April, in which practically all employees work eight hours, are paid for twelve hours, and turn the proceeds over to the United Fund. We have been doing this for fifteen years and each year have won the 100 per cent participation award. During coffee breaks on United Fund Day there are free coffee and doughnuts for everybody (so far, the record, held by one of our big fellows in the Shipping Department, is seven doughnuts).

The committee also functions as a team in the United Fund Drive, using company cars and company time for their work of solicitation.

The Better Government Committee, as such, does not involve itself in politics. It encourages all employees to pay their poll taxes and turn out for every election. The committee also urges employees to write to their senators and congressmen in regard to current issues. On one occasion, more than 100 letters went out, advocating economy in government.

The committee also makes recommendations to management regarding special programs for our Monday morning employees' meetings. Three or four times a year we invite an outside speaker, such as the Mayor, County Commissioners, the Sheriff, the District Attorney, FBI Agents, the Tax Collector, the Superintendent of Schools, State and Federal Judges and United States Congressmen, to bring us a message on some phase of government.

One of the best avenues for communication in a small or medium sized company is a periodical assembly of all employees. In our company, such an assembly is held every Monday immediately after the morning coffee break. The meeting lasts for about forty minutes: approximately one-half of the time is devoted to a business session; the balance is given over to the company chaplain who has charge of the religious service.

During the business session, we frequently have reports from one or more of the employee committees. Then one of the company executives will discuss some phase of the company's activities, such as fire insurance, fire protection, or safety (usually accompanied by slides or a movie); or how we keep track of the 5,698 different items in our inventories, or any one of a thousand similar subjects.

The president asks for reports on new babies. The

proud but often embarrassed fathers come forward to receive their checks for one day's extra pay and to give particulars over the microphone regarding the new arrival—whether a girl or boy, the name, weight, time of birth, and the health of the child and mother. In one case where twins were involved, the matter of extra pay was decided by a general referendum; the employees voted unanimously and vociferously in favor of *two* days extra compensation.

These business sessions, while usually serious in their content, nevertheless provide many occasions for good humor and laughter.

The religious part of our Monday morning meeting will be discussed in the chapter which follows.

FELLOWSHIP in the WORKING FAMILY

EARLY ONE MORNING, SEVERAL YEARS ago, we had an explosion in Dallas. It occurred about 4:00 A.M. and we were told later that people as far away as two miles from the scene of the accident were awakened from their sleep by the noise of the explosion. The Mitchell Company's reinforced concrete loading dock had blown up, mysteriously. The dock was about 10 feet wide, 4 feet high and 200 feet long. Its floor and front wall, together with the ground beneath, and the wall of the building to which the dock was attached, had formed the four sides of an open-end tunnel 200 feet in length. Apparently, gas from a faulty gas main under the street had leaked slowly into this tunnel, filling it with an explosive mixture that needed only a spark to set it off.

The spark had been supplied, no doubt by a cigarette butt flipped into one end of the tunnel by a careless passer-by, who, incidentally, must have been somewhat surprised at the immediate reaction.

We certainly were surprised when about 7:00 o'clock we arrived and surveyed the damage. The dock was completely broken up into hundreds of large, jagged fragments which were lying around, some on the railroad siding, some in the street and some merely up-ended and leaning against others.

Here and there could be seen the twisted, protruding ends of reinforcement rods.

Soon most of our working force had arrived at the scene. The men and women gazed in awe at the wreckage and talked to each other in hushed voices. All of us no doubt were picturing, each in his own mind, dead and injured men lying among and under the fragments. This would indeed have been the case had the explosion occurred during a lunch period or coffee break, for in good weather the dock was a favorite outdoor gathering place for a large number of our people. However, there were no deaths and no injuries, for the simple reason that no one was there at the time. The clean-up men had gone home four hours before the explosion, and the night watchman was in one of the other buildings when the accident occurred.

As we all stood there, looking and thinking hard, someone suggested that we ought to hold a prayer meeting to thank God for His providential care. This seemed to everybody to be a good suggestion, and by common consent, all four hundred of us went to the employees' assembly room and there began our workday with thanksgiving to our Heavenly Father for His goodness to us.

I don't remember whether or not anyone thanked Him for the explosion itself. Certainly we should have done so, since the explosion had drawn us all closer to the Lord and, as a result, closer to each other.

Because nothing is more effective for bringing people together than a sincere worship of God, we feel justified in spending fifteen or twenty minutes of each Monday morning in a worship service. After the business part of the meeting has been completed, the chaplain takes over for the religious part. He first reports on our sick folks, giving us what particulars he can regarding the illness in each case. Then he leads us in prayer in behalf of these friends, reads a passage from the Scriptures, brings us a brief message, and dismisses the meeting with a final prayer.

Our chaplain is about forty-five years old, and besides his regular education, has four years of seminary training. Perhaps most important of all, he has worked hard in our plant as a factory employee. Not many of us know what Tom's denominational background is. He is a staunch Christian, faithful to Christ and to God's Word. What does he "preach" about? Almost anything he pleases, so long as he avoids controversial subjects and is careful not to offend any Christian's viewpoint. We have among our employees Roman Catholics, Jews, Baptists, Seventh Day Adventists, Lutherans, Episcopalians, Pentecostals, Presbyterians, Methodists, Disciples of Christ, Church of Christ people, non-denominational independents, and no doubt others whom we do not know about.

The chaplain does not pull any punches when he talks to us, but so far as we are aware, in the nineteen years since we have had a chaplain, no personal offense has been given by his preaching.

An industrial chaplain has much the same responsibilities as an army chaplain. Besides proclaiming the gospel and exhorting those of us who claim to be Christians as to our Christian duties, he visits the sick, comforts the afflicted, counsels with those who have problems, conducts funeral services, to name a few of his activities.

I have gone somewhat into detail about our "religious" program and the industrial chaplaincy because, judging by our mail, there is currently a good deal of interest in the subject among certain industrial leaders.

Another unifying force frequently in evidence in an industrial organization is any good cause or project that enlists a common sympathy and makes possible a common response. For example, observe how almost everybody—in a department of a large company, or in the entire company if it is a small one—will rally to the help of any employee who has been the victim of a sudden misfortune. Someone suggests that a relief fund be raised and almost immediately the fund *is* raised. The folks do, voluntarily and collectively, what no one of them could do by himself. As a result, the experience draws the group closer together in a fellowship of service.

Once, before we had our credit union in the Mitchell Company, such a relief fund was quickly subscribed for assisting one of our boys who really stood in need of help. He had experienced a string of misfortunes, was broke and heavily in debt. Now his wife was hospitalized for an emergency operation. The employees got busy and not only raised and turned over to the young husband a considerable sum of money, but they also sent the Sick and Welfare Committee to the hospital to take some personal necessities to the wife. While there, the committee members got acquainted with an army sergeant who was sitting beside *his* sick wife in the same hospital room. The soldier looked so scared and so forlorn that the committee, after a brief investigation, came back to the factory to raise a fund for *him*. The next day they took *his* wife some similar presents. As they handed him their gifts, they were treated to the rare sight of a top sergeant with tears in his eyes. He was greatly moved as he thanked our folks for their kindness.

What interests me about the incident is not so much the atmosphere of gratitude and happiness that the Sick and Welfare Committee left behind them in the hospital room where the two women were patients, but the atmosphere of satisfaction and joy that the committee brought away with them. They and the folks they represented had gone the second mile, as the Saviour suggests. Naturally, one of the results of the experience was to draw all of the participants closer together by that "blessed tie" that binds Christians together in Christian love and service.

Very often extracurricular activities have a lot of fun connected with them. For example, there was Winkie Morrow at the Blood Bank. Winkie was and still is a very small person. Although quite healthy, she lacked a few pounds of weighing enough to qualify for blood donations. Winkie met this problem by hiding somewhere on her person a babbitt hammer and when she got on the scales she had a pound to spare.

Then there was the irrepressible Lynn Bennie who, after giving pint No. 8, went out through the exit door and immediately came back in through the entrance door in an effort to give pint No. 9 on the same day. Fortunately, he was recognized by the authorities who suggested that he return five weeks later.

Incidentally, the average for our entire organization was five pints per person.

Still another force that operates to draw employ-

ees together is the fellowship of sports and amuse-
ments. In the Mitchell Company, bowling, baseball,
basketball, and miniature golf tournaments, under
the auspices of our Sports and Entertainment Committee, have proved to be highly successful in this
regard. So was the ball game played at one of our
picnics with the cooperation, or rather the non-co-
operation, of eight trained donkeys, one for each
player except the pitcher and the catcher. Whenever
a batter hit a fair ball, he mounted his donkey and
rode, theoretically, at least, toward first base. Sometimes the animal would trot docilely halfway to the
base and then would pitch the rider over his head, or
perhaps would gallop off in the opposite direction, or
would simply freeze in his tracks until the ball, hit
for what otherwise would have been an easy home
run, was relayed two or three times to the first base-
man for a put-out. All of the spectators, and most of
the participants as well, agreed that never in all the
history of the world had there been so hilarious a
baseball game.

Our annual company picnic is one of the year's big
events. It usually takes place late in September, just
before the great State Fair of Texas opens for its
two weeks' exposition. The company leases the Midway for the picnic and from three to six o'clock all
of the rides and concessions are free to the employees
and their families. The younger men and women
have a great time on the roller coaster, the Wild
Mouse, the bumping cars, and the Ferris wheel.
Some of the older folks, who want to kid themselves
and their friends into thinking that they are younger
than they really are, take the same rides and pretend
to enjoy them.

The real fun, however, comes in watching the little tots as they ride the merry-go-round, the little boats, the miniature trains and the circle swing.

At six o'clock the twelve hundred people gather together and form eight "chow" lines. The blessing is asked, and ten minutes later all are busy putting away as much barbecued beef, fried chicken, and other good food as their several capacities will permit.

All the details are handled by the employees' Sports and Entertainment Committee. The members of this committee are very popular, and deservedly so, especially among the future Mitchell Company employees—the boys and girls.

A sure way to draw folks closer together is to let them have fun together.

Some reader may wonder whether, in view of all these extracurricular activities, we ever find time for work. We can assure him that we do. In fact, I think that we work with more enthusiasm and more devotion as a result of the three fellowships of fun, service and worship.

CHAPTER
17

WHAT KIND of MANAGER?

IF, AS EMERSON SAYS, "AN INSTITUTION is the lengthened shadow of one man," then obviously the top executives of American business enterprises are very important. They have it in their power to help or to hurt a great many people.

What traits of character do you think should be required, or at least hoped for, in an employer, a manager, the top executives?

We asked this question of two friends about a week ago, both of them employees of a Dallas company. We were so impressed with their replies that I am reproducing them herewith. What they say, while very discouraging to me personally as a manager, is interesting because they both speak from the viewpoint of employees.

WHAT AN EMPLOYER SHOULD BE

The head of a business concern should possess certain qualities which set him apart as a leader and clearly indicate his right to the position he holds. These are qualifications which should be recognized and cultivated.

A leader should possess real character, the result of a personal relationship to Christ. He leads best who best follows the Saviour. His qualities of leadership will be strengthened and fortified because of personal attention to spiritual realities. A man who sets an unwavering standard as a servant and follower of Christ will be able to operate from an unshakable foundation in every other area of life.

It logically follows that, as a man of Christian character, a good leader will also be a man of *integrity*. He will keep his word. He will be honest in his dealings. He will not shade, hedge or deviate in word or conduct. He will maintain his personal integrity even though it may involve great cost to himself.

The head of a business, in order to lead, must display *firmness*. Those he leads must know that he means what he says and that no trifling will be countenanced. Such firmness should, of course, stop short of inflexible stubbornness.

Impartiality should be another mark of leadership. Probably one of the most frequent complaints against a leader is that of unfairness. At all costs a person must be fair toward everyone with whom he deals. Decisions and conduct alike must not be influenced by personal considerations or personalities. People like to feel that they are receiving treatment equal to that accorded others. Therefore, every effort should be expended to justify and sustain that attitude.

Another ingredient of good leadership is the *ability to make decisions,* right decisions. There will be decisions which are the result of weeks and months of careful study and analysis. Decisions of another type offer little or no time for forethought. Perhaps these might be called "experience" decisions which, after all, do in reality represent preparation—the accumulation of a lifetime of knowledge.

The leader will be a man of *courage*. No true leade can be lacking in this quality. He will need courage not only to make decisions, but also to stand by them. He will need courage when criticized for his principles. He will need courage when confronted by manifold problems and burdens. He will need courage when tempted to take the easy way out.

An unusual attribute, perhaps, but one that should

be evident in a leader's life is *compassion*. This is not the antithesis of courage, but its natural complement. The leader must have a genuine, humble concern for the weak, the needy, the helpless, the poor, the sinful, the fallen.

A leader will be a man of *humor*. Life is serious and business unrelenting, and a sense of humor is a great help in relieving tension; it aids in gaining a true perspective in many situations. Life is not a big joke, but a good joke can make life more enjoyable for oneself and for others.

Appreciation of others will characterize the true leader. He will not be guilty of that meanest of the vices, ingratitude. There probably have been more bitter tears shed and more grievances aroused over lack of appreciation than can be charged to any other executive shortcoming. The faculty for noticing people, and deeds that often go unnoticed, is a rare and desirable virtue. The key to the undying and genuine loyalty of one's employees is gained through the constant and sincere exercise of appreciation.

An employer will *not* be *self-important*. Others will be important to him, but never he, himself. He will surround himself with people he trusts and will not be afraid to delegate to them the authority which their responsibilities require. He will never be so taken up with his own ways and ideas that he becomes blind to those of the people who surround him.

T. R.

Four Qualifications of a Business Leader

There are four qualifications which, although not often considered essential in a business leader, yet are of vital importance to his *real* success. We might call them the four P's.

In the first place, he should have the right *perspective*. It isn't as difficult to view the past in the right perspective as it is the present and the future. If first things are put first, the less important things will usually fall in place with little attention.

To be a true leader of men, one needs to have a proper perspective of the spiritual phase of life. Jesus said, "Seek ye first the kingdom of God, and his righteousness; and all these things [material things] shall be added unto you" (Matthew 6:33). Not only will such material things as are needed be supplied to those who put God and His kingdom first, but other characteristics essential to successful leadership will be added to the executive who has a proper perspective of spiritual things.

If God be given first place in a man's life, He will add much to that life; but nothing that is detrimental or degrading. ". . . all things work together for good to them that love God, to them who are the called according to his purpose" (Romans 8:28).

Another qualification a leader should have is *purity*. It would seem very difficult to view clearly the correct answers to important questions and pressing problems through a heart and mind clouded by impurity.

The wise man said, "For as he thinketh in his heart, so is he . . ." (Proverbs 23:7). The state of one's purity is determined by the condition of the heart and mind. Pure thoughts proceed out of a pure heart.

Purity begets confidence and faith. The Bible tells us that ". . . if our heart condemn us not, then have we confidence toward God" (I John 3:21). Purity also begets honesty; and no leader in business or any other area of life merits his position if he is not honest: honest with God, with himself, and with his fellow men.

Peaceableness is a quality which should be in evidence in a leader's life, both in conversation and actions. In a society often beset with unrest, ill will and discontent, a leader who is calm and not easily disturbed can have a stabilizing influence on those about him.

Many men are not at peace with themselves, nor with

one another, because they are not at peace with God. If
one is at peace with God, he has no reason to be fearful,
emotionally upset or apprehensive. Peace of heart brings
peace of mind—quietness, calmness and contentment. If
one reaches the state of perfect peace with God, the
turmoil and storm within will cease, just as the angry
waves of the Sea of Galilee subsided when Jesus spoke
to them and commanded them to be still. There is
nothing that can quiet the nerves and remove tension
caused by fear, worry and the cares of life, like the voice
of the Saviour.

A peaceable man is considerate of others. He does not
go around with a chip on his shoulder, but delights in
assisting those who need his help.

A good leader is *purposeful* and energetic. He has a
purpose in life; a goal to attain. And he has the ambition
to diligently pursue that goal until it is attained. Although the leader is peaceable, yet he is forceful, resolute
and determined. He does not deviate from his purpose
because of greed, selfishness, pride or the opinions of
others.

The life's purpose of a leader should be, not primarily
to make money, nor merely to gain honor, fame and
prestige for himself, but to honor and glorify God, do
His will and serve his fellow men to the best of his
ability.

N. W.

After reading these two papers several times, I cannot but wish they had been available forty-five years
ago, at the outset of my business career, rather than
now near the end of it. I could have put the advice
to good use had it been available then, during many
troublous times and in numerous hours of decision
of the kind that every executive is frequently called
upon to face.

CHAPTER
18

A GREAT DISCOVERY—
THE BOOK

SURELY IT WOULD BE DIFFICULT TO conceive of anything more exciting or rewarding than to make a great discovery—a discovery that would have a far-reaching effect upon multitudes of people still living and upon generations yet to come.

We can imagine, for example, the great thrill that must come to an archaeologist who unearths an ancient civilization which has been buried for hundreds of years, and thus adds a new chapter to the records of history. Or the excitement of an explorer who, after overcoming obstacles and hardships to reach some almost inaccessible part of the earth, looks for the first time on a new body of land or a new river.

Think of Euclid and his amazing discoveries in the field of elementary mathematics and geometry! Think of Galileo who with his own hands made a celestial telescope and looked out into the night and beheld vast oceans of stars never before seen by man! Think of Newton as he came into some of God's own secrets regarding the laws of motion and gravitation! Think of Fabre as he discovered those amazing facts, one after another, about the insect world! Think of Anton Leeuwenhoek, the Dutch shopkeeper and janitor of the seventeenth century, who, as a hobby, ground finer lenses than anyone had ever made before and then looked through them at a new microscopic world—a fly's leg, a louse's eye, a drop of water. Hear him as he calls excitedly to his daughter: "Come here! Hurry! There are little animals in this water . . . they swim! They play around! They are a thousand times smaller than any creatures we can see with our eyes alone. . . . Look! See what I have discovered!" Leeuwenhoek the janitor, later a Fellow of the Royal Society of London, had discovered in a single drop of water a whole new world —the world of microbes—and had thus laid the foundation for much of modern medical science.[1]

To be a pioneer on any frontier and to make discoveries that will affect the lives of future generations must be exciting business, indeed. But I am bold enough to claim that every Christian has made three great discoveries which transcend, in their importance to him, any discovery that has been made or conceivably can be made in any field whatever. These three discoveries are based upon assumptions so breathtaking in their concept as to be both blasphemous and preposterous, if it were not for the fact that they are ratified and encouraged by God Himself:

1. God has written us a personal letter.
2. God loves each one of us, personally.
3. God wants each one of us, personally, to love Him.

I shall concern myself at this time only with the first discovery.

Many years ago, I received a letter from a marquis in whose chateau in France I had been privileged to be billeted during the First World War. His letter

[1] See Paul deKruif, *The Microbe Hunters,* (New York, Harcourt, Brace & Co., Inc., 1932).

was a simple note of congratulation upon my forth-
coming wedding. I prized this letter so highly, coming
as it did from a lineal descendant of one of the kings
of France, that for the next year or two whenever
we had guests in our home I would steer the conversation around to the point where it would seem natural
to introduce the letter; then I would trot it out and
read it to my bored friends.

How ridiculous! Even if the letter had come from
King Louis XIV, how insignificant as compared with
a personal letter from God Himself! How infinitely
more important it is to have received a communication from the Creator, the One who made the heavens
and the earth—and me!

But how can this be? How can one justify the as-
sumption that God has written a personal letter to
each Christian? Why is the Christian convinced that
the Bible is, in effect, a series of letters, assembled in
a convenient package which we call the Bible? Why
does the Christian believe that the Bible is indeed
God's Word? And why does he feel that it is intended
specifically for him?

There are many proofs of the divine authorship of
the Scriptures. Here I shall refer to only two.

1. God alone can have such knowledge concerning
our characters as is disclosed in the Bible. "For the
word that God speaks is alive and active: it cuts more
keenly than any two-edged sword: it strikes through
to the place where soul and spirit meet, to the inner-
most intimacies of a man's being: it exposes the very
thoughts and motives of a man's heart" (Hebrews
4:12, PHILLIPS). The Bible tells us things about ourselves that only God can know.

2. The Bible is unique among all the world's

literature in that it alone *claims* to be the Word of
God. Everywhere we turn in the Old Testament, we
read such phrases as, "Thus saith the Lord," "The
word of the Lord came unto the prophet Isaiah saying . . ." and many similar expressions. And in the
New Testament we read: "But you must understand
this at the outset, that no prophecy of scripture arose
from an individual's interpretation of the truth. No
prophecy came because a man wanted it to: men of
God spoke because they were inspired by the Holy
Spirit" (II Peter 1:20, 21, PHILLIPS).

Then in II Timothy 3:16 we come upon this statement: "All scripture is given by inspiration of God
and is profitable for doctrine, for reproof, for correction, for instruction in righteousness."

These declarations, and a hundred others like
them, come out of the pages of this Book to convince
us that it is indeed the Word of God.

But how do we know that the Bible is intended for
us, personally? Why can we claim that God has sent
these communications to us, individually? Are they
not intended for everybody? Of course they are—at
least in one sense. But in another sense, they belong
to each one of us. I think every Christian who loves
this Book has the feeling that it was written especially
for him. He finds in it answers that fit his needs so
perfectly that he has a right to say that God has
spoken to him, expressly and directly.

A good example is old Mr. Tate. Mr. Tate lived
alone in a frame house not too far from our factory.
Just how I became acquainted with the old gentleman I do not now remember, but he and I became
fast friends. I used to visit him during the noon hour
and chat with him about the Civil War, about cur-

rent events and particularly about the Lord. Mr.
Tate possessed a Bible which had seen so much use
that it looked less like a book than a collection of
loose leaves in a binder.

One day Mr. Tate expressed a desire to attend one
more meeting of the local Confederate chapter. The
meeting was to be on Sunday afternoon in a public
hall about two miles from Mr. Tate's home. I volun-
teered to take him there in my car.

When we arrived at the meeting place, it was apparent that the old man was too weak to climb the
steep stairs. However, since he weighed scarcely a
hundred pounds, it was no problem to scoop him up
in my arms and carry him up the steps.

The other veterans were already there, about eight
of them, sitting around a table. The rays from the
late afternoon sun were slanting in through a nearby
window and falling like a benediction on their white
heads. I put Mr. Tate down in the chair that had been
reserved for him, and took my own place among the
relatives at the other side of the room.

After the business session was completed, Mr. Tate
asked for the floor. In a very touching little speech,
he told his comrades that he expected this would be
his last meeting with them; that his old body was
getting pretty tired, and he hoped that before long
he would be going home to be forever with his Lord
and Saviour. He expected to attend other meetings
with his friends in heaven, and therefore his present
good-bye would be for only a little while. A little
while, indeed, for after a few weeks he left us and
went home to the Lord.

Of the few items of personal property he left, it
was the Bible, worn by time and tattered by use, that

disclosed the secret of his life. The Book there on the table beside his bed spoke with quiet eloquence, confirming by hundreds of marked passages that it had been a lamp unto his feet and a light unto his path.

To the old gentleman, it was not a book, it was The Book.

We need God's Word in business. The executive needs it particularly to be his source of wisdom and courage, his constant inspiration, the rule of conduct for his life. Let him, therefore, have a Bible on his office desk, or close by, not for a showpiece or a talisman, but for a book of reference. If he is wise, he will refer to it regularly—perhaps each morning as he begins his day.

Let the Book remain in its place, and it will cause strange and wonderful things to happen as people come and go, in the course of business.

THE GREAT NEED

WHAT IS WRONG WITH AMERICA today?

Nothing, say the ostriches. Nothing is wrong with America at all, they say.

Truly, an incurable optimist is as wrong as an incurable pessimist. Both are dangerous counselors. The one will not take his head out of the sand and look about him, because he is afraid of what he may see. The other is so fascinated with the gloomy things which he does see, that he is unable to find, or even to seek, a way of escape. The one says that the patient is not sick, that there is no such thing as sickness; the other says that the patient is going to die, because there is no remedy.

Almost we feel like shouting with Mercutio, "A plague o' both your houses!"

For an objective, unbiased, up-to-the-minute view of America today, I refer the reader to some words which are now about 1900 years old. They are contained in a brief letter written by the Apostle Paul to his young friend Timothy. Let me quote just one sentence from this letter: ". . . in the last days perilous times shall come. For men shall be . . . lovers of pleasure, more than lovers of God" (II Timothy 3:1-5).

America today has many gods, but her favorite is the goddess Pleasure.

What is the cure, the remedy, for our disease? For the answer, I again refer the reader to the Scriptures, this time to a passage dictated by the Holy Spirit to an unknown Hebrew chronicler almost 2900 years ago, as a warning and a promise for all posterity: "If my people, which are called by my name, shall humble themselves, and pray, and seek my face, and turn from their wicked ways; then will I hear from heaven, and will forgive their sin, and will heal their land" (II Chronicles 7:14).

The great need of America today is for us to return to the God of the Bible; to repent of our sinful and silly ways; to throw ourselves upon the mercy of God; to accept *His* way of salvation; and then to endeavor so to live our lives as to please the Father in all that we say and do and think.

That way lies happiness for us, and the consummation of the optimist's most cheerful dreams. The other way, the way we are headed, lie dispair and ruin and the complete fulfillment of the pessimist's most dismal forebodings.

God give us the good sense and strength to heed His warning and to seek His promise, while there is yet time.

CHAPTER
20

CHRIST at WORK
AMONG WORKERS

THERE CAN BE NO QUESTION ABOUT IT
—the most effective and the happiest business organization, all other things being equal, is that company whose employees are God-fearing people.

This is not to advocate a hiring policy that would discriminate between believers and unbelievers, or one that would show favoritism for any race or religion. However, I am convinced from many years of firsthand observation that a company whose management is governed by Christian ideals will eventually be a Christian company. The reason for this is simple. An enterprise with a Christian management naturally attracts people who prefer to work in a so-called Christian atmosphere. As a result, there will always be a strong nucleus of earnest, God-fearing employees, and these folks, not so much by precept as by their happy example, will soon draw others to their way of life and to their Lord and Saviour.

One of the most exciting aspects of my business experience has been to observe the Lord at work in the lives of my friends in factory and office. I have seen alcoholics win miraculous victories over this dread disease and sin. I have seen selfish men become unselfish, actually concerned about the welfare of others. I have seen people who were formerly inclined toward shady practices become, as Christians, truly honest men. I have seen men who *without* Christ would have gone to pieces under some great trial but who, *with* Christ, have triumphed over it and have become all the stronger because of the test.

So far as I know, those employees of our company who have accepted Christ as their own Lord and Saviour were never subjected on our premises to any high-pressure evangelism. No one here, I am sure, has ever seized them by the coat lapels and demanded of them: "Are you saved?"

However, they have been subjected to the quiet but powerful influence of Christian lives which testify to God's transforming grace—lives lived by people working alongside them whose daily walk is with the Lord Christ Himself. How could one work in the same department with folks like E. S., or J. I., or A. S., or R. P., or J. H., or G. A., or F. S., or a hundred others I can think of, and not be impressed with their attitude toward life and their joyous, purposeful way of living it? These people go through the same trials that the average non-Christian does, but each test seems to result in a new victory. They too get sick, like everybody else, and have their disappointments and sorrows; but such experiences, instead of sending them to the pill bottles and the psychiatrist's couch, seem to draw them nearer to God.

These Christians know their Bibles and can say with the psalmist: "O how love I thy law! it is my meditation all the day" (Psalm 119:97). They feel a great dependence upon their Heavenly Father and know how to talk to Him about their problems, failures and successes—we have heard most of them do it. They are kind and gentle. They are concerned and compassionate. They are enthusiastic and dedicated. They have peace of mind and poise.

Were they always like this? No. Their lives have been changed. They have different attitudes now than they once had, different loyalties and purposes, different likes and dislikes. One characteristic, common to them all, is a deep, singing type of joy, come weal or woe, in place of the fears and worries that once possessed them. They have moved off the throne themselves and have turned the control of their lives over to a new Sovereign, the Lord Jesus Christ. Each of them is ". . . a new creature: old things are passed away; behold, all things are become new" (II Corinthians 5:17). A miracle has been wrought.

Now, any non-Christian who witnesses this miracle and perceives its continuing effects day after day is likely to be curious and to make inquiries as to its nature and cause.

If he does, *he* will be introduced to the most important—infinitely the most important—Person it will ever be his privilege to know, Christ Himself. Only let the inquirer open *his* heart, and the Lord will come in to be his Redeemer, his Master and King, his Counselor, his Friend. Christ promises: "Here I stand knocking at the door; if anyone hears my voice and opens the door, I will come in and sit down to supper with him and he with me" (Revelation 3:20, NEB). And so our friend becomes a Christian, too. Soon he too will be a living testimony to the grace and power of Christ.

No buttonholing, no harangues, no arguments. Just another miracle!

A FRIEND TAKES
the WITNESS STAND

To CONCLUDE THIS BOOK, I HAVE ASKED
a close friend to take the witness stand for direct
questioning. This friend is likewise a manufacturer,
himself the president of a company, an inventor, an
engineer, a Christian. The questions are mine, the
answers are his.

QUESTION: When and where were you born?

ANSWER: I was born the first time April 4, 1903, in
St. Louis, Missouri.

QUESTION: What do you mean by "born the first
time"?

ANSWER: Life began for me in 1903, and it was life
with God-fearing parents, for which I am grateful.
But it was a temporary life, in a temporary body,
subject to disease, rebellion, sin, death and judgment.
"For all have sinned . . . ," the Scriptures tell me. And
". . . the wages of sin is death. . . ." "And as it is
appointed unto men once to die, but after this the
judgment" (Romans 3:23; 6:23; Hebrews 9:27).

A large part of my life had passed before I saw
Jesus Christ as the marvelous Person that He is.
When I did see Him, an overpowering sense of guilt
and inadequacy came upon me. I longed to know
Him, in the same way that little Zacchaeus had

longed to know Him. (Luke, Chapter 19). Nobody had to tell Zacchaeus he was a sinner. Nobody had to tell me, either. The time came when I realized that Christ had been seeking me! He loved me personally! He longed to save me from my sins and to be my Lord, to take over as the King of my life!

So I opened the door of my heart and let the great Redeemer come in. A new life began then and there —a new *kind* of life. It is a life of purpose, peace and joy. He calls it "eternal" life. And He says that this new life must begin with a "new birth" (John 3:7).

Thanks to God's amazing grace, I have been permitted to find this out for myself, and to be born the second time.

QUESTION: What is a Christian?

ANSWER: One in whom Christ lives. As He put it, "If a man love me, he will keep my words: and my Father will love him, and we will come unto him, and make our abode with him" (John 14:23).

QUESTION: What do you think of Christ? Who do you think He was, or is?

ANSWER: The only One by whom I know God. "Shew us the Father," said Phillip. Jesus replied: " . . . he that hath seen me hath seen the Father. . . ." The Apostle John, who was closer to Jesus and knew Him better than anybody else, said He was the Word who was with God and who was God—the very expression of God Himself (John 1:1-14). "And the Word was made flesh, and dwelt among us, (and we beheld his glory, the glory as of the only begotten of the Father,) full of grace and truth." His main purpose in coming was to be our Saviour.

QUESTION: What do you mean by Saviour?

ANSWER: The very name Jesus means Saviour. Even

when He arrived on this earth, "born of a woman," instructions were given that His name should be called Jesus, "for he shall save his people from their sins." When Jesus went home with Zacchaeus, His critics murmured, saying, "That he was gone to be guest with a man that is a sinner," but Jesus' reply was: "The Son of man is come to seek and to *save* that which was lost" (Luke 19:2-10). It is no wonder that we find Peter, Paul, John, the angels, Mary and the men of Samaria all calling Him the Saviour (Acts 5:31; Philippians 3:20; I John 4:14; Luke 2:11; Luke 1:47; John 4:42).

QUESTION: Do you believe in a life hereafter? If so, why?

ANSWER: Certainly, because of the Lord's statements and because of His own demonstrations.

To Martha, one of a family of the Lord's close friends, He said, "Whosoever liveth and believeth in me shall never die . . ." (John 11:26). To the penitent thief on a cross next to The Cross, He said, "To day shalt thou be with with me in paradise" (Luke 23:43).

Every time one of the words *forever, eternal,* or *everlasting* is used in the Scriptures, it is an assertion that there is life hereafter. For example, "For we know that if our earthly house of this tabernacle were dissolved, we have a building of God, an house not made with hands, eternal in the heavens" (II Corinthians 5:1). There are hundreds of similar references in the Scriptures.

By way of demonstration, Jesus Christ waited until Lazarus had been in the tomb long enough for his body to begin to decompose; then He called, and the soul of Lazarus responded. The Lord reunited the soul with the body, and Lazarus walked forth.

Later, Christ made the *great* demonstration with His own body, when He Himself walked forth from the tomb, no longer subject to death. He appeared in His resurrection body to numerous witnesses on many different occasions, convincing even the doubtful, and then ascended into heaven (Acts 1:10-11).

QUESTION: What advantage is there in being a Christian other than the hope of eternal existence in heaven, wherever that is?

ANSWER: The last half of that question reminds me of an answer given by a young friend of mine in his first class in college. The question the prof had asked was, "Is there anyone in this class who thinks he knows where he is going when he dies?" In the total absence of any response from the other students, my friend held one finger up about halfway. But the prof poured it on, "Just where, young man, do you think you are going when you die?"

A surge of courage was provided, as the youngster replied, "I'm going to the place prepared for me by my Lord Jesus Christ, and I don't care where it is."

This young man was given a fine Christian wife, and together they faced life full of confidence in their Lord. He is now having a great time teaching high-school youngsters, and she is having just as much fun raising three children of their own. Of course, they find the usual problems and troubles confronting them, but also they have found that life's problems are solved and life's difficulties are overcome in the presence of Christ. Real love, real joy and real peace are fruits produced only by trust in the Saviour.

All who *do* put their trust in Him can say, "My

God supplies all my need, according to his riches in glory by Christ Jesus" (Cf. Philippians 4:19).

QUESTION: Is it your idea that everybody "needs" Christ? If so, why?

ANSWER: Yes, indeed. Personal need is supplied by a Person, not by any kind of ethical code, or legalistic procedure. And our vital and supreme needs can be supplied only by One Person, the Lord Jesus Christ. Only He can forgive our sins and remove our guilt (II Corinthians 5:21). Only He can make good on a promise to be present with us through sorrows and troubles of all sorts (Deuteronomy 31:8). Only He can understand our frailties, and provide the strength we need (Philippians 4:13). Only He can save us: save us from ourselves, save us from spiritual death, save us from the power and penalty of sin, save us from despair, save us from ignorance concerning realities that matter, save us from every obstacle in the way of a full, joyful, purposeful life. The life with Him has for its great motive the simple desire to please the Lord Jesus Christ, now and forever (Acts 4:12; Colossians 3:23).

To this I say, "Amen!" and briefly add my own testimony.

I would rather be a dead cat in an alley than a man possessed of perfect health, boundless power and vast wealth, favored with popularity and blessed with countless friends, *but without Christ*. For a dead cat has the virtue of being, once and for all time, dead; whereas a man who has rejected the grace of the Lord Jesus Christ is not only dead now—dead in unforgiven "trespasses and sins"—but must face two other kinds of death: physical death, which is the separation of the body from the soul, and eternal death, which is everlasting separation from God.

Not by any fancied righteousness of my own—not by any sweet kindnesses or "good works" which I may have performed—but only by the grace of God and the redeeming power of Christ, am I a Christian. Like all other Christians, I have the assurance of God's Word that my sins are forgiven; that I am an heir of God, and co-heir with Christ; that one day He shall take me to be forever with Him in the place that He has gone to prepare for all those who put their trust in Him. Because the Lord is *my* Shepherd too (John 10:10-16) I can say, along with all other believers, "Surely goodness and mercy shall follow me all the days of my life: and I will dwell in the house of the Lord for ever."

Someone reading these affirmations will say, "This fellow is a dreamer of dreams." If so, I would like to ask, what harm can there possibly be in dreaming a dream that is so helpful and so thoroughly practical?

It may be that some other reader, not quite so critical, will say: "This fellow is at least sincere. He believes what he says. Perhaps I ought to do a little investigating of these claims for myself."

If you are such a one, I offer you both a challenge and a promise.

The challenge is that you first read the Gospel of John three times, prayerfully, studiously and with an open mind; and then read the entire New Testament.

The promise is this: if you will conscientiously fulfill the terms of the challenge, then, whoever and whatever you may be, God will speak to *your* heart. You will come to realize that Jesus Christ is God; that He came to the earth to be your Saviour, that He loves you infinitely more than anybody else does or possibly can; that He longs to be your unseen but intimate Friend, "closer than hands or feet," your Counselor and your Sovereign.

In other words, you will wake up to make the astounding discovery that all other believers have made before you, that this is no dream, after all, but a wonderful reality—more real and abiding than test tubes, bank vaults, wage checks, astronautical rockets, planets and stars. You will be a new man, with a new life, a new purpose, a new peace, a new assurance, a new and abiding joy.

As far as your vocation is concerned, you will discover a new satisfaction in doing all things "heartily, as to the Lord, and not unto men." You will have discovered that to be a Christian in business means to be in business with Christ.

To this wonderful Person, the living Son of the living God, our Lord Jesus Christ, be all the praise and honor and glory, now and forever!